SEWING SCHOOL

21 Sewing Projects Kids Will Love to Make

Amie Petronis Plumley & Andria Lisle

photography by Justin Fox Burks

Storey Publishing

The mission of Storey Publishing is to serve our customers by publishing practical information that encourages personal independence in harmony with the environment.

Edited by Deborah Balmuth and Cindy A. Littlefield
Art direction and book design by Jessica Armstrong
Text production by Liseann Karandisecky

Photography by © Justin Fox Burks
Pattern diagrams by Missy Shepler

Indexed by Catherine Goddard

Storey Publishing
210 MASS MoCA Way
North Adams, MA 01247
www.storey.com

Printed in China by R.R. Donnelley
10 9 8 7 6 5 4

Library of Congress Cataloging-in-Publication Data

Lisle, Andria.
 Sewing school / by Andria Lisle and Amie Petronis
Plumley ; photography by Justin Fox Burks.
   p. cm.
 Includes index.
 ISBN 978-1-60342-578-0 (paper w/concealed wire-o and flaps : alk. paper)
 1. Sewing—Juvenile literature. I. Plumley, Amie Petronis. II. Title.
TT705.L56 2010
646.2—dc22
                                                          2010022154

Dedicated to our mothers, Suzanne, Betty, and Debby,
who taught us our love of sewing firsthand.

ACKNOWLEDGMENTS

Without the talent and enthusiasm of the Sewing School campers at Memphis' Grace-St. Luke's Episcopal School, this book would not have been possible. These campers — and all of the kids who sewed, laughed, and shared their ideas with us — gave this book life.

Most of all, we thank our own families (Amy Lawrence, Cassius Lisle, and Eric, Phoebe, and Frank Plumley) for their love and patience, especially during the months that we talked about *Sewing School* nonstop!

We are deeply grateful to the following people: Kevin Barré, who made us look good in our author photos; Millett Vance and Gene Rossetti at Flashback; Dr. Karnes and the staff at Central Animal Hospital; Lickety Split ice cream man Joe Patty; and Bill York, who happily provided locations and props. Headmaster Tom Beazley, the administration, staff, families, and students at Grace-St. Luke's Episcopal School for the use of their campus and for their support and wonderful inspiration. Especially

Katie Donald and Libby Shannon, who allowed us to test patterns and offered a multitude of ideas during Sewing Club.

We'd also like to thank Deborah Balmuth and Alethea Morrison and everyone else at Storey Publishing for believing in us and helping guide our vision to fruition; the readers of our Sewing School blog, who share our passion for sewing with kids; and Robert Gordon, Tim Duggan, and Doug Halijan for offering their expert advice as we navigated our publishing contract.

CONTENTS

GIVE

WEAR

RECYCLE & REPAIR

VET CLINIC

A NOTE TO YOU FROM THE AUTHORS

Hi! We're so glad you're excited about *Sewing School*. When we were young like you, we couldn't wait to learn how to sew and make things all by ourselves.

When Amie was a girl, she was lucky because her mom taught her how to sew. Amie especially liked to make her own outfits. She learned how to sew buttons and add patches to vintage clothes that she bought at the thrift store. One day, Amie wore a skirt she made by wrapping a piece of fabric around herself and fastening it with safety pins!

Andria's mom also sewed. At Christmas, Andria could always find homemade stuffed animals and dolls under the tree. Every spring, she would help pick out a pattern for the dress her mom would magically whip up by the time the Easter Bunny came around. After Andria learned how to hand-sew using her mother's scraps, she started making blankets and pillows for her teddy bears.

Now that we're all grown up, we sew even more. After college, Amie started sewing again because she couldn't find cute clothes. Today, she sews skirts for herself; pajamas for her husband, Eric; clothes for her kids, Phoebe and Frank; and toys for her two cats. Amie also teaches kindergarten and runs an after-school sewing club for her students.

Andria loves to sew new pillows for her home and blankets for her dog, Cassius. Last Christmas, she practiced sewing with her niece, Maclin. Andria works at an art museum and often looks for unusual fabrics from around the world.

In our spare time, we like to teach children how to sew. Every summer, we hold a Sewing School day camp at Amie's school. These campers, ages 5 to 13, tested all of the projects in *Sewing School*. They also modeled for our friend Justin, who took the photos in this book.

We love sewing with kids. You already know that it's easy to sew — you just want to learn how to use a needle and thread so you can create stuffed animals, make presents for your families, and play veterinarian by mending your own toys. The patterns in this book are very basic, because we know that you have the imagination to "make it yours" as you go.

Writing this book was very important to both of us because we want kids everywhere to be able to learn how to sew. Now, you don't have to attend Amie's school, or wait until next summer rolls around to enroll in our camp. You can learn how to sew whenever you want, right inside your own home.

We hope that you will love sewing as much as we do. And we hope that someday — maybe soon or perhaps later on — you'll help teach other kids how to sew, too!

XOXO *Amie + Andria*

Amie Petronis Plumley & Andria Lisle

An Introduction for Adults

Sewing School inspires and teaches children how to sew, using step-by-step directions, simple language, and child-created examples of contemporary sewing projects suited for a modern home.

Once kids learn a few basic skills, they'll be eager to try their hand at all kinds of sewing projects. This book builds on prior knowledge using "step-up projects" that employ developmental cues established by the Montessori and Waldorf schools. For each project, we've included A Note for Grown-Ups to identify steps that require adult assistance. The directions themselves are written at a second-grade comprehension level, with projects designed for sewers ages five and up.

Sewing School isn't as rigorous as a home-economics class. During our hands-on sewing sessions with younger children, we've discovered that, for the most part, young sewers don't care about pressed seams and neat hems. So we decided to focus on easy, fun projects that don't require extra work. That said, most intermediate sewers will naturally take these projects to the next level by initiating additional steps on their own.

For kids who aren't quite ready to handle a needle and craft thread, start out by showing them how to lace sewing cards. Or help them sew an easy shape (try the So Soft Pillow on page 47 or the Cute Coasters on page 86) by

holding the fabric pieces taut and then lifting them up to chest level so kids can see both sides of the fabrics as they guide the needle and thread. We've done this successfully with four-year-olds who desperately want to sew like their parents or older siblings.

Almost all of the projects in this book are hand sewn. Still, children are often fascinated by sewing machines. If this is the case with your child, try moving the pedal to a tabletop so he or she can press it with one hand to

make the needle go. Demonstrate how to raise and lower the presser foot and how to gently guide the fabric while you remain in control.

You'll find more basic sewing machine guidelines in Lesson Six: Get Your Stitch On (see page 24). If you're looking for a kid-friendly sewing machine, we recommend buying a basic adult model rather than a toy. We like the sturdy and practical Janome Sew Mini Sewing Machine (see Resource Guide, page 141).

Getting Started

Regardless of your own ability, your child can sew. All you need to do is provide a few inexpensive tools, such as kid-friendly needles and thread and a pair of scissors. Refer to the Resource Guide (see page 141) for a full list of our tried-and-true recommendations.

Of course, you'll need fabric, too. While you can easily purchase fabric at retail stores and online, you can also find it around the house in the

form of outgrown clothing and cast-off sheets and pillowcases. Kids will probably need help initially threading needles and making knots, but other than that, they can sew with minimal supervision.

As children learn to sew, they improve their fine motor skills and learn how to focus and follow directions. In fact, during our summer camp sessions, we've been astonished to discover that children who were previously bouncing off the walls were more than willing to sit down in a quiet place so they could focus on their projects.

Before your child starts sewing, please discuss sewing safety (see Lesson Four: Sewing School Rules on page 19) with your young sewer, and invest in the tools we recommend in Lesson Two: In Your Sewing Kit (see page 14), which are sized just right for kids' hands. Also be sure to stress the importance of asking for adult help when needed. And provide a quiet place to sit and sew, as well as a few plastic bags with zipper-type closures to store works in progress.

Once they start sewing, some children will repeatedly ask midproject, "What's next?" Refer your sewer back to the book, which has detailed written and photographed steps. Resist the urge to continually rethread needles or tie knots yourself. Instead, guide your child through the directions in Lesson Five: Ready, Set, Thread (see page 20) to help teach self-sufficiency.

Encourage Creativity

Whether on purpose or by accident, kids often go off on a tangent during the crafting process. When sewing, encourage your kids to add their own personal touches if they like. We've included a list of ideas entitled Make It Yours for each of the projects in this book. By learning that they can complete a project in different ways, kids will gain more confidence in their abilities and take their imaginations to new levels.

One way to promote creativity is to encourage young sewers to use recycled materials. See what your kids can make from a discarded pillowcase or the buttons cut off a too-small shirt. Ask them to help with mending, or let them update their old clothes with fabric embellishments.

Finally, remind young sewers of this rule for sewing: nothing has to be perfect. Flaws are more than okay, they're endearing. Imperfections give each project a unique flair that cannot be found in mass-produced merchandise. It's also important to remember that sewing projects don't have to be finished in one sitting. The most important thing is just to have fun!

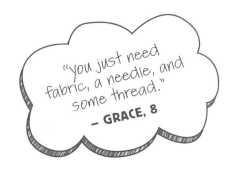

"You just need fabric, a needle, and some thread."
— GRACE, 8

Sewing with a Group

When we initially decided to teach Sewing School as a summer day camp activity, our friends thought we were crazy. We wondered, too, as we faced the roomful of 30-plus first- to fifth-grade students, many of whom had never sewn a single stitch. Yes, it was daunting — but we learned that sewing can be a fun group activity, viable for classrooms, birthday parties, or after-school sessions.

As with any successful project, you need to plan ahead. Make sure you have the right supplies and tools on hand. Prethread some needles. You'll need to provide flat surfaces for cutting and sewing, too. During summer camp, most of our kids sewed at group tables, while a few others preferred to flop on a beanbag or into a comfortable chair.

Don't feel dismayed if some kids don't maintain interest in the chosen project. Some might be perfectly happy draping themselves, toga style, with pieces of fabric, while others will race to the finish with oversized stitches. We've taught kids who, once they made their first So Soft Pillow (see page 47), stayed on that trajectory for the full week, making dozens of pillows in every color and size. We've seen young sewers who start out with a basic pattern like the Hold-My-Stuff Bag (see page 65), then deviate from our design to add their own pockets, flaps, and handles. We've also had kids make completely adorable Your Little Friend dolls (see page 53) and then render them unrecognizable with fabric markers and crayons.

Remember, it's okay if they go off track. Sewing is about what *they* want to make, a celebration of their creativity. Oftentimes, the results are amazing. Here are some tips for staying organized when sewing with a group.

* **Set up different stations around the room**: one area for needles and thread, another area for fabric, and yet another for stuffing. Place bowls of notions on each table.

* **Stock plastic bags** with zipper-type closures in a big bin. Kids can use them to store their works in progress.

* **Discuss sewing safety**, at the beginning of each day. (See Lesson Four: Sewing School Rules on page 19.)

* **Put up detailed step-by-step project directions** on the chalkboard or bulletin board, and have a sample of the final project on hand.

* **Make multiple copies of the pattern** using poster board and a marker. Keep them near the project directions, preferably at the front of the room.

* **Offer simpler activities for nonsewers**, if possible. You might provide weaving tools and supplies, for example, or a bowl of beads to string.

* **Have blank paper and drawing materials available** so kids can create their own patterns and sketch ideas.

* **Assess the abilities of sewers in a multiskilled group** by making So Soft Pillows (see page 47) or Stuffies (see page 49). Some kids might not progress beyond this point, which is okay, as long as they continue to have fun.

Clean Up

While it's not difficult to instruct a roomful of young sewers, the scene can often look chaotic. Try appointing helpers who, at designated times, are responsible for picking up specific items:

* **Needle monitors**, armed with magnetic wands, can pick up spare needles and pins.

* **Stuffing supervisors** are responsible for reorganizing the pillow-stuffing station.

* **Material managers** can refold fabric and return it to the proper place and pick up small scraps off tables and the floor.

* **Take a break after a cleanup**, by reading to the group from a sewing-themed book (see Story Time on page 61).

Sew and Tell

At the end of the day, have a show-and-tell time for young sewers who can discuss the designs and techniques they used to put their own stamp on their sewing projects. Encourage sewers to explain which experiments worked best, and compare and contrast different variations on similar projects. Invite parents and friends to attend.

Start Sewing

During your sewing session, encourage independence, and remind young sewers that nothing has to be perfect. Here are some tips for making sure kids have the information they need to become self-sufficient.

* **Show first-time sewers how to thread needles on their own**, using a LoRan needle threader and working in small groups. Once students have mastered this task, have them make paper badges and staple them to an accomplishment bulletin board in the room.

* **Demonstrate the basic sewing steps necessary to complete a project.** We like to break the kids into small groups and teach specific skills such as threading needles, sewing stitches, and tracing patterns. Use the lessons in the Getting Started section (see page 11) as a guide.

* **Before starting on a particular project, talk about its usefulness.** Ask kids for ideas about variations. Discuss which fabrics they might use.

* **Ask more experienced sewers to assist their less-skilled counterparts.** Remind first-time sewers that if they run into problems, they can carefully undo their stitches and start again.

* **Have the kids make their own Book of Needles** (see page 39) for a first project. Ask them to personalize their needle books in some way or use masking tape and a permanent marker to put their name on the back. Remind your sewers to always return needles to their needle books after sewing.

Welcome to Sewing School!

Do you know how to sew? Maybe you've already made something with a grown-up or a grandparent, or used a needle and thread to sew on a loose button. Or maybe you're brand new to sewing and can't wait to get started.

This book is filled with fun projects you will love to sew. And all of them have already been kid-tested by sewers from 5 to 13 years old.

Before you jump into sewing, please take some time to read this chapter all the way through. It's filled with all kinds of helpful tips for sewers — like what tools you should keep in your sewing kit and how to choose the right material for your fabric masterpieces.

Here are some other sewing skills you will learn about in this chapter:

* how to thread and knot your own needle

* how to sew a running stitch and a whipstitch

* how to sew on a button

Most importantly, you will learn how to sew all on your own!

"Sewing is not impossible."
— NIA, 7

"I learned how to do the whipstitch!"
— ELLIE, 6

How to Use This Book

Sewing School is written for young sewers ages 5 and older. It is filled with step-by-step pictures and directions that make it easy to learn how to sew. We've added tips to make sure that everything goes smoothly so you have lots of fun. Here are the kinds of tips you'll find with each project.

Ratings

Each project is rated with one, two, or three stars so you will know the skill level needed to complete it. If you are a brand new sewer, you can start with the easier projects and work your way up. The ratings work like this.

One star means it is an easy project. It is perfect for new sewers. You will sew, at most, two pieces of fabric together. You can make an easy project in about an hour.

Two stars means it is a skill-building project. You will get to try out some new skills, such as sewing on a button or adding some trim. You might want to spend all afternoon or even a few days on this type of project until you get it done.

Three stars means it is a harder project. These projects are meant to challenge you. They have more steps than the other projects, and they might take days or even a week to sew.

Let's Review

This is a short list of the skills you'll need to complete the project. You might want to go back over the lessons included in this chapter before you begin.

A Note for Grown-Ups

This is a message for your parent or another adult who might be helping you sew the project.

What You Need

This is a complete list of the fabric and supplies you will need to complete the project. You will find many of those supplies in your sewing kit. (See Lesson Two: In Your Sewing Kit on page 14.)

Make It Yours

All of the projects in the book are very basic. It is up to you to make them special. Here, you'll find a few ideas for putting your own stamp on a project.

SEWING SCHOOL RULES

New and expert sewers always follow these four basic rules.

1. At all times, know where your needle is!

2. Be safe.

3. Remember that nothing has to be perfect.

4. Take your time.

In Your Sewing Kit

Kids' sewing kits are very similar to grown-up sewing kits, but they're not exactly the same. You will have more fun sewing if you have the right kid-sized tools. These tools don't cost very much money, and as long as you take care of them, you will be able to use them for a long time.

Here is a list of what you will need for your sewing kit. You can find more information about these tools in the Sewing Dictionary and the Resource Guide in the back of this book.

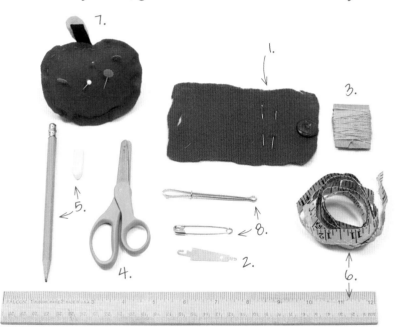

1. **Chenille Size 22 Sharp Point Needles.** Your needles will be your most important tools for sewing. A needle has a hole, called an eye, on one end and a point on the other. You don't want to misplace your needle — it can hurt if you accidentally get poked with one. Keep all of your needles safely stored in your sewing kit.

2. **LoRan Needle Threader (for large-eye needles).** A needle threader is a tool that will help you get the thread through the eye of the needle. Be sure to keep your needle threader with your spare needles.

3. **Craft Thread.** Craft thread is what you will use to sew your fabric. It comes in many different colors. It is also called *nondivisible fray-resistant cotton floss.*

4. **Scissors**. Scissors are an important part of your sewing kit. You will use them to cut fabric and thread. We like Fiskars for Kids scissors. Never cut paper with your sewing scissors — this will make them dull. Scissors cut fabric best when they are sharp.

5. **Chalk and Pencil**. Use chalk or a pencil to trace patterns and measurements onto fabric. Chalk works great because you can rub off any extra lines after you're done cutting.

6. **Ruler or Measuring Tape.** A ruler or measuring tape will help you measure exactly where you need to cut and sew. A ruler works best when you are working on a table or on the floor. Keep a measuring tape handy for measuring people, pets, or items that aren't flat.

7. **Pincushion and Straight Pins (with large, round heads).** Straight pins come in handy when you need to pin a pattern to your fabric or hold two or more pieces of fabric together. Keep them nearby in a pincushion.

8. **Bodkin or Large Safety Pin.** Either of these will be useful when you are making a casing or pushing elastic or string through a long, narrow fabric pocket.

Find the Perfect Home for Your Sewing Kit

Now that you have the supplies you need, you need something to put them in. Here are some ideas.

1. Recycle a school supplies box or a cigar box. Ask an adult to help you decoupage it with Mod Podge and old sewing patterns. Or cover an empty oatmeal carton or shoebox with wrapping paper or pages from a magazine.

2. Make your own Get-to-Work Apron (see page 79) with just the right-sized pockets for your sewing supplies and a little pincushion.

3. Sew an extra large Draw-It-Up Tote (see page 70) and store it inside a basket.

4. Search a thrift store — or, with permission, a grown-up's closet — for an old purse, a briefcase, or a backpack.

5. For a well-organized kit, use a fishing tackle box or toolbox to sort your tools and supplies.

Finding Out about Fabric

Learning how to choose the right material, or fabric, is very important. Sometimes you need a certain fabric to make a project in this book. Other times you can pick any kind of fabric you like.

Keep in mind that the colors and patterns of the fabric you use can tell the whole world how you're feeling. Fabric can also give clues about who you are or what you like. Maybe you want to use fabric printed with cats to make a Just-Right Pouch (see page 74), or maybe you'd like to sew your dad a red, white, and blue Too-Hot Holder (see page 92) to use at a Fourth of July cookout. Use the Resource Guide in the back of this book to find out where to buy all kinds of printed fabric. Or design your own using muslin and fabric markers!

With a grown-up's permission, you can shop for fabric right inside your own house. Ask if you can have old sheets and pillowcases, towels, or even tablecloths for your fabric stash. Maybe you've outgrown clothes you can cut up to make something new. Just be sure to ask first!

If you're buying new fabric, keep in mind that most of the projects in this book call for fabric that's about the size of a sheet of paper. A ¼-yard piece is a good amount to buy, unless you are making a big project like a skirt or an apron.

Here are some popular fabrics that were used to make the projects in this book.

* **Felt.** Felt is a great fabric to have around. It is thick and colorful and bright on both sides. Most felt comes from sheep's wool, although some felt is man-made. The important thing to remember about felt is that it will not fray — when you cut it, there are no loose threads that you have to hem or sew down. Felt usually comes in squares that are just the right size for the projects in this book.

* **Fleece.** Fleece is like felt, but it's softer and not as scratchy. A lot of times, fleece is made from recycled plastic water bottles! Be sure that your needle is sharp when you're sewing with fleece, because pushing a needle through this thick fabric can be tough. At the fabric store, ask if they have any small pieces of fleece on sale. Wash fleece before you sew to make it really soft!

* **Cotton.** Cotton fabric is easy to cut and sew, but it frays, or fringes, when you cut it. If you buy cotton fabric, ask a grown-up to wash it before you use it, because it might shrink a little bit. Afterward, cotton fabric might need to be ironed. If so, ask a grown-up for help.

FELT

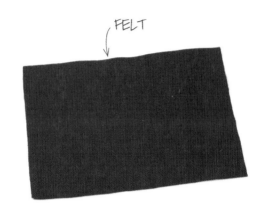

FLEECE

COTTON

"I like sewing because you get to use cool fabric. My favorite patterns are polka dots and hearts, and my favorite colors are blue or green or red or gray."
— ANNA MERCEDES, 8

KEEP IT TIDY

Fold up all your fabric so it stays organized. Maybe you have a shelf or a bin you can keep your fabric in. Get another bin for small scraps, which you can use to decorate your finished projects or use as stuffing in a pinch.

THE RIGHT CUT

Make sure you have a pair of scissors that are used *just* for cutting fabric. If you use these scissors on paper, they'll be too dull to cut the fabric well, which can get very frustrating. Keep in mind that whether you're cutting out a small piece or a big pattern, you want to start at one edge instead of cutting from the middle of the fabric. And if you're cutting cotton, stop and make sure you know which side of the fabric is the good side. For patterned fabric, make sure the design is going the right way or it might end up upside down!

Most cotton fabrics have two sides — a front and a back. Pay attention to the front, or *good* side, of the fabric when you're cutting and sewing, and be careful to keep the good side of the cotton on the outside of your project. The good side of the fabric is the one where you can see the print really well. On the other side, the print looks faded.

Sometimes you put the good sides out. Here, the elephants are brighter on the good side. When you sew, you can see all of your stitches.

When you don't want to see the stitching, you put the good sides together. The medals are brighter on the good side. Then you turn what you are sewing good side out.

Fabric stores sell cotton fabric by the yard (3 feet of material at a time). At many stores, you can buy as little as ⅛ yard. Or ask if they sell *fat quarters*, which are ¼-yard squares of cotton fabric used by quilters.

* **Muslin.** Muslin is a thin cotton fabric the color of oatmeal. If you want to use crayons or fabric markers to draw designs or a pattern on the fabric, muslin is a great choice. Try drawing your picture or pattern on paper first, then trace it onto the muslin with a pencil. It helps if you tape the fabric down to the table before drawing on it. Like cotton, muslin frays, but it doesn't have a good side.

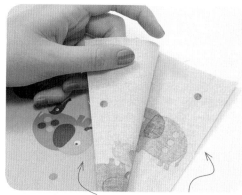

Here the good sides face out.

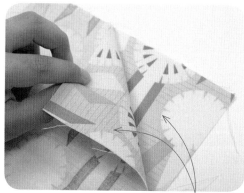

The good sides are together.

MUSLIN

Sewing School Rules

You already read these Sewing School Rules on page 13. Here are the reasons behind them.

1. Always know where your needle is!

This is very important. Just like a grown-up's needle, your needle is sharp and will hurt if it accidentally pokes someone. Never put a needle in your mouth! Take the time to make a needle book (see page 39) to keep in your sewing kit. If a needle does poke you, be sure to wash the spot with soap and water, and ask a grown-up to check you out.

2. Be safe.

Find a good place to sit and sew. This can be in your bedroom, a chair in the den, or an out-of-the-way spot in the kitchen. Wherever you go, don't walk and sew! And be sure to check in with a grown-up whenever you need to use an iron, or when a project calls for adult help.

3. Nothing has to be perfect.

What you sew might not look like stuff you could buy in a store, but that's okay, because you made it yourself. Most sewing mistakes are easy to fix. You can undo your stitches just like you can erase a line that you made with your pencil. Simply take off the needle, put it in your needle book, and carefully pull your thread loose; then start over. See page 28 for more ideas about how to fix a project that's gone wrong.

4. Take your time.

None of these projects have to be completed in a single day, or even a week or a month. Sewing is not a race, so try to relax. When you want to take a break, store your project in a plastic bag that zips closed.

"Even if you're a beginner sewer and you mess up, it still looks really cool. And if you really mess up, you can easily change your idea to something else."
– MARGARET, 9

Ready, Set, Thread

Now it's time for one of the most important steps in sewing: choosing and measuring the thread and then threading your needle.

How to Make a Bobbin

Before you start sewing with your craft thread, you need to wind your thread onto bobbins. This is easy and fun to do, and it will keep your thread from getting tangled up.

What color of craft thread do you want to sew with?

1 First, cut some old cardboard (empty cereal boxes work great) into rectangle shapes that are about 1 inch wide and 2 inches long. Do *not* use your sewing scissors for this!

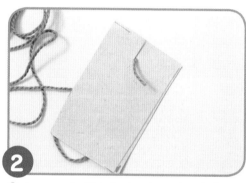

2 Cut a small slit into both ends of the bobbin. Slide the tail of the thread through the slit in one end.

3 Wind, wind, wind until all the thread is on the bobbin. Then tuck the loose end into the other slit. Now your thread is on a bobbin.

Measure the Thread

We like to use the Arm Length Rule when cutting thread. No matter how young or old you are, if you follow this rule, you will always end up with the perfect length of thread.

1 Measure the thread from your shoulder to your hand.

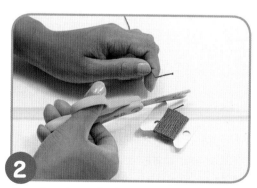

2 Cut the thread where you measured.

Thread Your Needle

Try using a needle threader to get the job done. We like the LoRan Needle Threader.

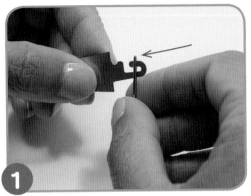

1 Put the hook of the threader through the eye of the needle.

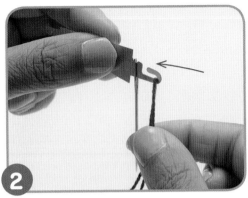

2 Hook the thread.

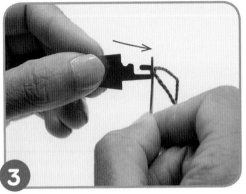

3 Pull the needle off the threader.

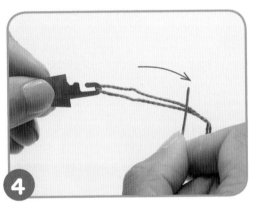

4 Keep pulling along the thread.

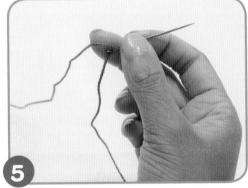

5 Unhook the thread. The needle is threaded. It's magic!

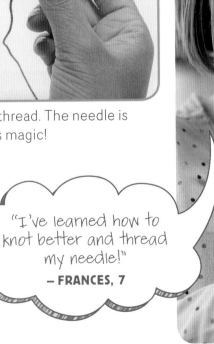

"I've learned how to knot better and thread my needle!"
— FRANCES, 7

Anatomy of a Needle

1. This is the *eye*, or hole, in the top of the needle. Use a needle threader to help you pass the thread through the eye, then position the needle a little more than halfway down the thread.

2. This is the *point*. Use this end to guide the thread in and out of the fabric.

3. This is the *thread*. The knot at the end will keep your stitches from coming undone.

4. This short end is called the *tail*. Always keep the tail a little shorter than the knot end of the thread.

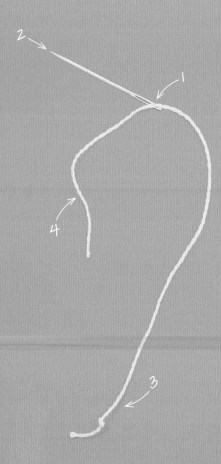

"you just have to try your best on this. You'll never know you can do it unless you try."
— MARY, 9

Now, Tie a Knot

Once your needle is threaded, you need to knot the end of the thread to keep it from pulling through the fabric when you sew.

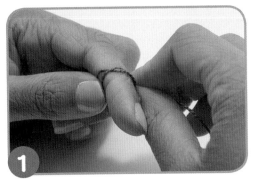

1 Wind the end of the thread around your finger.

2 Slip the thread off your finger. You made a loop.

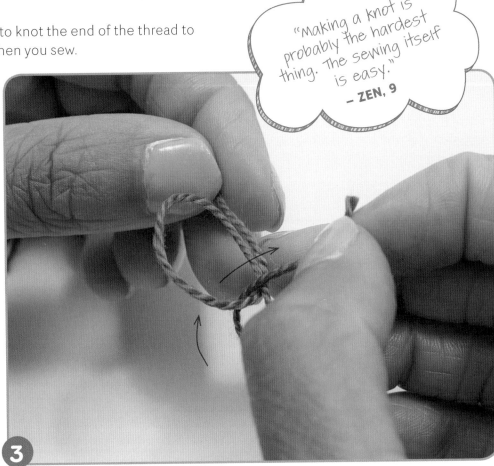

3 Bring the short end of the thread up through the loop.

4 Pull tight. You made a knot! Use the same steps to make a knot when you are finished sewing or run out of thread. Do not cut the thread until you make a knot!

Get Your Stitch On

Your needle is threaded, and you have a knot tied at the other end of the thread. Now you are ready to sew your first stitch! Here are two kinds of stitches you will use to sew the projects in this book.

How to Sew a Running Stitch

The running stitch is the most basic sewing stitch. Use it to sew two pieces of fabric together or to embroider a picture or a design. When it's done right, the running stitch looks just like a dotted line.

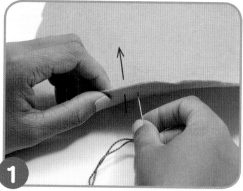

1 Push the needle up through the back of the fabric.

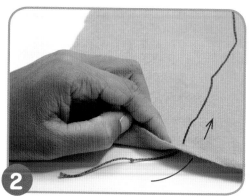

2 Pull the needle and thread until the knot hits the back of the fabric.

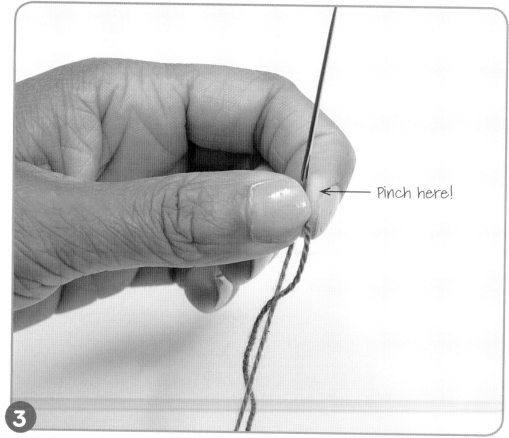

Pinch here!

3 Pinch the needle at the eye when you pull each stitch through. This way, the thread will not come out of the needle.

How long is your stitch?

If it is too big, it will leave open spaces in your sewing.

4 Push the needle down through the front of the fabric. Stitches should be about as wide as your thumbnail.

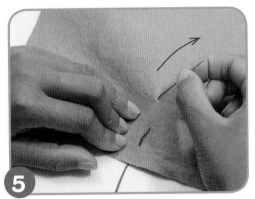

5 Bring the needle back up. Leave a little space between the needle and the last stitch.

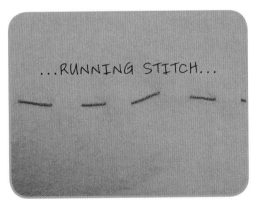

...RUNNING STITCH...

Keep sewing. You are doing a running stitch!

What If You Run Out of Thread?

Don't worry! Just start again. When you know you are going to run out of thread, be sure to stop sewing while you still have enough thread left to make a knot. If you don't have enough left, unthread the needle and pull out a few stitches. Once you've knotted the end, you can start sewing again with a new piece of thread.

"Sometimes, you run out of thread and you have to start over. You have to be patient!"

— EVA CLAIRE, 6

1 Make a knot at the end of your first thread. Cut any extra thread.

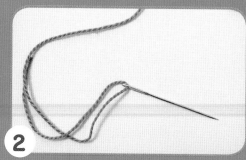

2 Thread your needle with a new arm's length of thread. Make a knot at the end!

3 Start sewing a new stitch right where you left off.

How to Sew a Whipstitch

The whipstitch is another easy stitch. Use it to sew two pieces of fabric together close to the edge. Or whipstitch a single fabric edge to decorate it and to help keep the material from fraying.

1 Push the needle up through the back of the fabric.

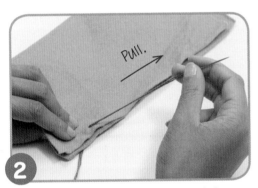

2 Pull the needle and thread until the knot hits the back of the fabric.

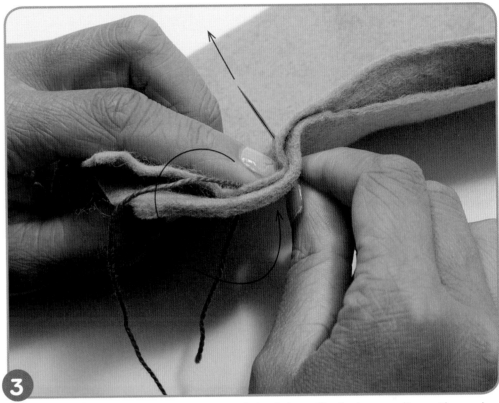

3 "Whip" your needle around the edge of the fabric. Push the needle up through the back of the fabric.

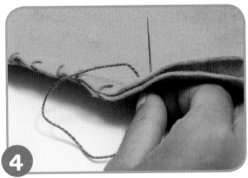

4 Make even stitches, only sewing up through the back of the fabric.

5 This is a great whipstitch!

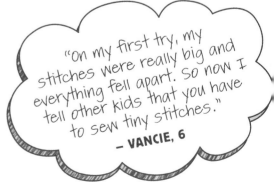

"On my first try, my stitches were really big and everything fell apart. So now I tell other kids that you have to sew tiny stitches."

— VANCIE, 6

Oops! Something Is Wrong!

It's easy to fix your stitches — even easier than erasing a line on paper. If you mess up, all you need is a pair of scissors and a new piece of thread to get back on the right track. When you see a problem, stop, take a deep breath, and think about how you might fix it. Now you can get to work. Here are some of the things that might happen when you are sewing and the ways to fix them.

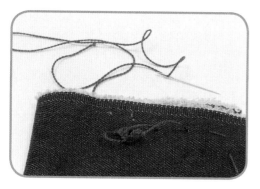

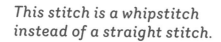

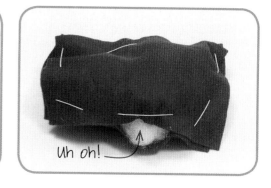

This thread is tangled.

Cut it close to the tangle. You might have to take out a few stitches so you can carefully make a knot. Cut a new piece of thread and start sewing again. Remember the Arm Length Rule!

This stitch is a whipstitch instead of a straight stitch.

Take the needle off the thread, so it's easy to undo the stitch. Rethread the needle and sew some more. Hint: You cannot sew backward.

The stuffing is falling out.

It's because the stitches are too big. Rethread your needle and sew between the stitches. Next time, make smaller stitches.

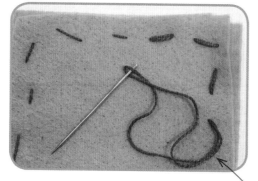

doubled up thread

"Once I sewed a pocket onto the wrong side of a skirt, and I just said oops!"
— MARGARET, 9

It's the wrong size.

These fabric pieces aren't the same size. If the sides don't match up when you put the fabric together, trim the bigger piece to the size of the smaller one. If you're making something to wear, you might have to redo the piece that's the wrong size.

This thread got doubled up.

Let go of the needle and carefully work the tail end of the thread out of the stitches. Be careful! Reposition your needle on the thread and keep sewing. Or cut the thread at the needle and make a knot. Then start sewing with a new piece of thread.

Sewing Machine Basics

You will not need a sewing machine for most projects in this book, although you are welcome to machine-sew if you already know how. Please remember that although you can sew much faster when you use a machine, you need to take your time. Get to know your machine before sewing a hard project. We recommend that you practice by making a So Soft Pillow (see page 47) or Cute Coasters (see page 86).

Here are some tips for when you're using a sewing machine.

1. For the patterns in this book, the seam allowance (see page 140) is ¼ inch or the width of your presser foot.

2. Take time to pin together the fabric before sewing. Stop before you get to a pin. Then take it out and put it back in your pincushion.

3. To turn a corner leave the needle in the down position so that it is in the fabric. Lift up the presser foot, and turn the fabric. Then put down the presser foot and continue sewing.

4. Backstitch at the beginning and the end of a seam (sewing backward for a couple of stitches and then forward again). This will knot the thread.

5. After you're done sewing a seam and knotting the thread, cut the loose threads close to the fabric.

"Sewing with a machine makes it go faster but can be tricky."
— **TESS, 9**

Patterns Down Pat

Before using the patterns that come with this book, you will have to cut them out. Cut the paper on the solid lines — remember not to use your sewing scissors here!

Once your patterns are cut out, you can store them in the back of this book. You can also copy them or trace them to make new patterns. If you want to make your own patterns, try using cardboard, cardstock, or a brown paper bag that is too thick to tear.

Once you've picked a project to make, find all of the pattern pieces. Read how many times you will have to cut out the fabric, and keep this in mind when choosing which fabric you want to use.

Smooth out your fabric on a flat surface (the kitchen table or a wood floor works great). Place the pattern on top of the fabric near one edge. Use your chalk or a pencil to trace around the pattern. It helps to pin the pattern to the fabric first. Or you can ask a friend to help hold down the pattern. If you don't have a helper, use a heavy can to hold your pattern and fabric near one edge. in place.

The patterns in this book were designed with a seam allowance of ¼ inch. This is the space between your stitches and the edge of your fabric.

"Without a pattern, your cutting is all crooked."
— CAROLINE, 8

Button Up

Buttons are very important. They are fasteners that can hold our clothes together or help keep a bag or a pocket closed. Buttons can also serve as an eye or a nose for a stuffed animal. Here's how to sew on two different kinds of buttons.

How to Sew a Flat Button

Flat buttons have two, four, or five holes for you to stitch through.

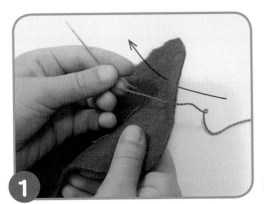

1 Bring the needle up through the back of the fabric.

2 Slip the needle through one of the buttonholes. Slide the button down the thread to the fabric.

3 Sew down through another buttonhole.

4 Sew through all the buttonholes at least two times. This way, your button will not fall off.

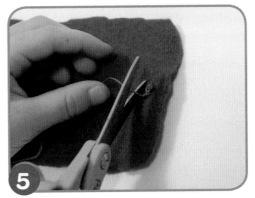

5 Push the needle to the back of the fabric and make a knot. Cut the thread.

How to Sew a Shank Button

Shank buttons have a metal or plastic loop on the back.

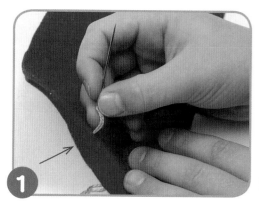

1 Bring the needle up through the back of the fabric.

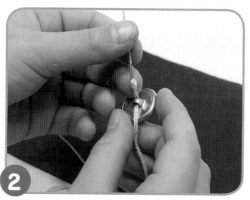

2 Slip the needle through the loop on the back of the button.

3 Slide the button down the thread to the fabric. Then put the needle back down into the fabric close to where you came up.

4 Now go back through the button two more times so your button will stay put. Bring the needle back up close to the button.

5 Slide the needle through the button loop.

6 Sew down through the fabric next to the button.

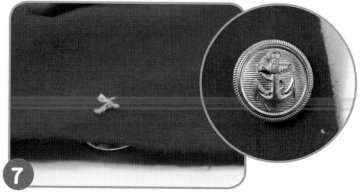

7 Make a knot in the back of the fabric. Cut the thread.

The button is sewn on!

"Sewing a button can take a lot of practice. Sometimes I get my grandmom to help."
— MARGARET, 9

Bring Your Project to Life

Every project in this book has basic sewing steps. During the sewing process, it's also important to "make it yours" by sewing on notions and trims. You might get some ideas from the pictures in this book, or you might dream up something completely new.

Craft stores are filled with all kinds of notions such as buttons, beads, googly eyes, ribbons, trims, pompoms, patches, and other fun stuff that you can add to your project. Most notions can be easily sewn on, but some can also be glued. Be sure to use craft glue made for fabric (see the Resource Guide on page 141 for more information).

Make It Special

Here are some ways you can turn an ordinary sewing project into something that's one of a kind.

* **Use iron-on patches** made for mending to create a special design. Cut shapes out of the patches with scissors. Then ask a grown-up to help with the ironing.

* **Personalize your project** with press-on letters, fabric markers, or crayons. Show off with your name, or draw a portrait directly on the fabric. If you're using crayons, you'll need to set your image into the fabric afterward. Ask an adult to help you with this! You'll need to turn the iron to a high setting and then carefully place your work on the ironing board. Make sure the fabric is smooth. Cover

"When I see something I made, I'm like, 'I made that!' and it feels pretty good."
— KENDALL, 8

it with a blank sheet of paper. Iron the paper for a few seconds, until the heat of the iron melts the crayon wax into the fabric. Let the fabric cool before you use it!

* **Use buttons, ribbons, rickrack, fabric scraps, and other notions** to make a face and a tail for projects like Your Little Friend (see page 53) or Quiet Mouse (see page 88). Give some personality to your project! Make it smile or frown. Follow the instructions on page 31 to add big buttons for eyes. Afterward, you'll need to add stuffing to fully bring your project to life.

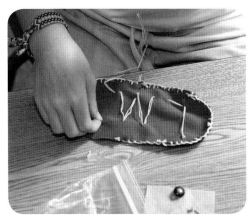

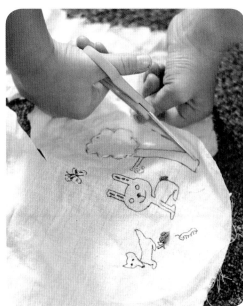

* **Sew some trim** onto your Hold-My-Stuff Bag (see page 65), or glue on patches to decorate an Eye-See-You Case (see page 90). It's fun to add trim to your work. The sky is the limit!

* **Embroider a picture of your initials** on a project like a So Soft Pillow (see page 47). Draw your design on fabric with a pencil. Now trace the lines with your needle and thread. It's just like drawing with your needle!

How to Sew on Trim

A little bit of trim can really dress up a simple sewing project. Here's how you put it on.

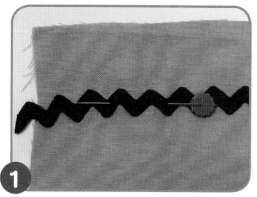

1 Pin the trim onto the fabric so it will stay in place while you sew.

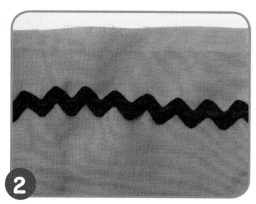

2 Carefully sew a running stitch down the middle of the trim. Small stitches will help the trim to stay on better.

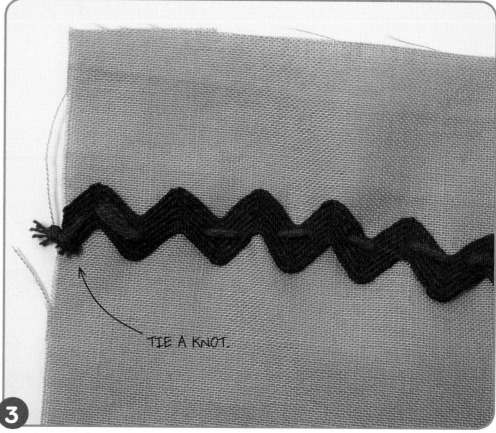

TIE A KNOT.

3 Tie a knot at the end and cut the thread.

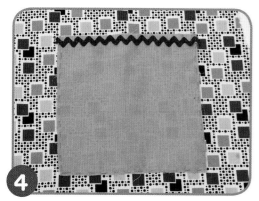

4 Look how nice this pocket looks with trim along the top.

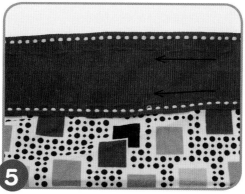

5 If the trim is wide, sew along both edges.

Stuff It!

Some sewing projects, like pillows and dolls, need to be stuffed. This is easier than you think. You can buy stuffing at a fabric store or craft store. Sometimes stuffing is man-made. Sometimes it's created from eco-friendly bamboo or cotton. No matter what it is made of, stuffing is usually white and as light and fluffy as a cloud. You can also make your own stuffing, using small fabric scraps that you might otherwise throw away.

1 When the pillow you are sewing is ready to stuff, take the needle off the thread. Take a small handful of stuffing.

2 Push the stuffing all the way inside the pillow.

3 Keep adding more stuffing until the pillow is filled up. You want a pillow that feels just right — not too hard or too soft.

STUFFING SKINNY PLACES

When you have to stuff small spaces like a doll's arms and legs, use something long and thin to help you push. We like using chopsticks or the eraser end of a pencil. Carefully push the stuffing into the small space. Use just a little stuffing at a time. Take your time and your doll will turn out fine!

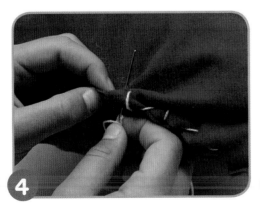

4 Rethread the needle. Sew the opening closed with the same stitch you used to sew the pillow. This pillow is sewn with a whipstitch.

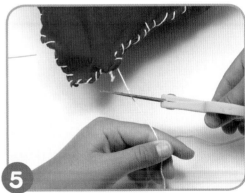

5 At the end of the opening, make a knot and cut the thread.

Making Casings

Sometimes when you're sewing, you need to make a casing. This is a long, narrow pocket that you pull elastic or ribbon through. One of the projects in this book that needs a casing is My Very Own Skirt (see page 110). The casing and the elastic make the skirt's stretchy waistband.

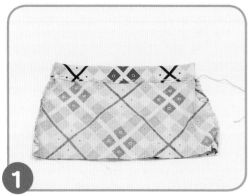

1 First, you need to leave an opening in the casing to pull the elastic through. It should be about 2 inches long. Here is a casing on a doll skirt. The opening is on the side.

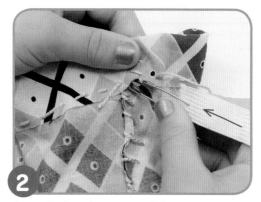

2 Attach the elastic or ribbon to a large safety pin or a bodkin. Push the safety pin into the opening in the casing.

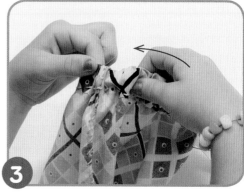

3 Use your thumbs to push the safety pin through the casing. The fabric will bunch together as you do this.

Pinch pin. Pull fabric.

4 Gently pinch the safety pin where it is inside the waistband to hold it in place. Then pull the bunched fabric over the elastic or ribbon.

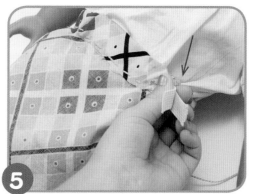

5 Repeat steps 3 and 4. Keep going, and pretty soon the top of the safety pin will come out of the opening. You want to end up with both ends of the elastic or ribbon sticking out of the casing.

WHAT'S NEXT?

For the projects in this book, the directions will tell you what you need to do once the ribbon or elastic is through the casing.

Pop Quiz

Now that you've had your sewing lessons, it's time to put your skills to the test. Here are two projects to make for your sewing kit. If you can follow the instructions, you'll get an A⁺!

A BOOK OF
NEEDLES

APPLE
PINCUSHION

"Try something easy first, then go to a project that's a little bit harder."

– GRACE, 8

A Book of Needles ☆

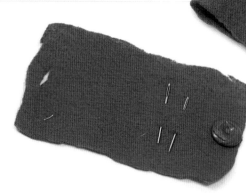

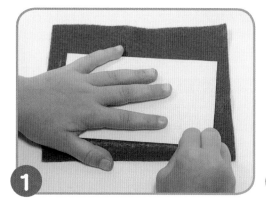Keep your needles safe and sound inside.

What You Need

- x Pattern for A Book of Needles
- x Felt scrap
- x Chalk
- x Scissors
- x Button
- x Sewing needle
- x Thread

LET'S REVIEW

Before you begin, you'll need to know how to:

sew on a button (see page 31)

A NOTE FOR GROWN-UPS

While this is a simple project, young sewers might need help sewing on the button, particularly if this is the first time they've done it. Another option is to make the book without a button.

1 Find the pattern piece in the back of the book. Use chalk to trace it onto the fabric one time.

2 Cut out the felt piece with scissors.

3 Now add a button. Sew the button onto one side of the felt. Sew it to the middle of the side.

4 Fold the felt over the button.

GO TO NEXT PAGE →

MAKE IT YOURS

* Add "pages" to your book by sewing two books together.

* Embroider the front.

* Sew a pocket inside to hold your needle threader.

* Skip the button and the book will still be fine.

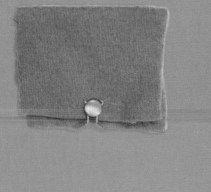

5 Use chalk to mark the felt on top of the button.

6 Fold the felt on the chalk mark. Cut along the chalk mark to make a buttonhole.

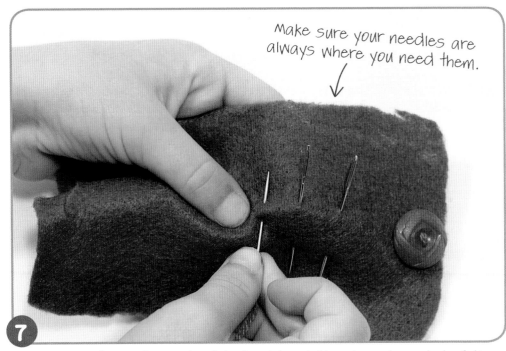

Make sure your needles are always where you need them.

7 Add your needles to the inside of the book by sticking them through the felt.

Now you can close the book and button it up!

Apple Pincushion ☆

If you stick your pins in a pincushion you'll know right where they are when you need them.

LET'S REVIEW

Before you begin, you'll need to know how to:

sew a running stitch (see page 24)

stuff a pillow (see page 36)

A NOTE FOR GROWN-UPS

This is a good first project. Sewers might need help when it comes to sewing through all the layered pieces of felt.

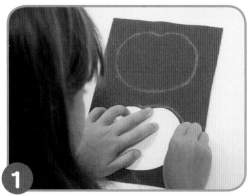

1 Find the pattern piece in the back of the book. Use chalk to trace it onto red felt two times.

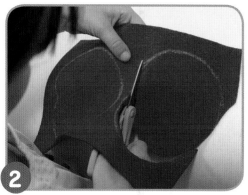

2 Cut out the two felt pieces.

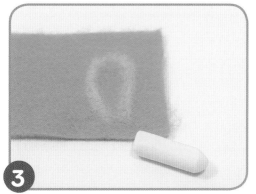

3 Draw a leaf shape on green felt with chalk.

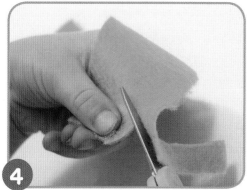

4 Cut out the felt leaf.

GO TO NEXT PAGE

5 Draw a stem shape on black felt with chalk.

6 Cut out the felt stem.

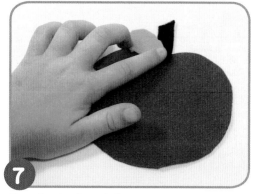

7 Put the leaf and the stem on one of the felt apples.

TIP: Pin the felt pieces to hold them together.

8 Put the second apple on top of the first one with the leaf and stem in between.

9 Time to sew. Push the needle through all the pieces of felt at the top of the apple.

Don't forget to leave an opening!

10 Sew around the edge with a running stitch. Leave an opening for stuffing the apple.

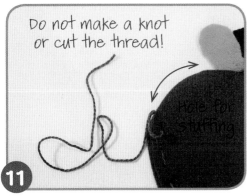

11 Take your needle off the thread. Put your needle in your needle book to keep it safe until you need it again.

12 Stuff the apple.

13 Rethread the needle. Sew the opening closed. Now make a knot in the thread. Then cut the thread close to the knot.

This cute apple pincushion is just the right size to fit in your sewing kit.

14 Time to put pins in your apple and add your pincushion to your sewing kit.

Happy sewing!

MAKE IT YOURS

* Change the color — now it's an orange!

* Use cotton or fleece fabric.

* Change the shape and make a new pincushion, such as a banana or an eggplant.

* Use it as a fun little pillow instead of a pincushion.

"You can sew your own stuffed animals. They're so cuddly that you can sleep with 'em."

— VANCIE, 6

HUG

You can sew up something to cuddle with in no time by following the instructions for the projects in this chapter. Tell a secret to Your Little Friend, or hug your So Soft Pillow close. When you are happy or sad, excited or scared, your creations will always be there for you when you need them most.

☆ **SO SOFT PILLOW,** *page 47*

☆ **STUFFIES,** *page 49*

☆☆ **YOUR LITTLE FRIEND,** *page 53*

☆☆☆ **TAKE-IT-WITH-YOU BLANKET,** *page 55*

☆ *easy*　☆☆ *medium*　☆☆☆ *hard*

So Soft Pillow ☆

You can never have enough pillows!

What You Need

- x Pattern for So Soft Pillow
- x Cotton fabric, ¼ yard
- x Chalk
- x Scissors
- x Pins
- x Sewing needle
- x Thread
- x Stuffing

LET'S REVIEW

Before you begin, you'll need to know how to:

whipstitch (see page 27) or *sew a running stitch* (see page 24)

stuff a pillow (see page 36)

A NOTE FOR GROWN-UPS

This is a perfect beginning project. Young sewers may need help threading a needle and knotting the thread. Once they've mastered sewing a basic pillow, they can have fun trying their hand at all kinds of variations.

1 Find the pattern piece in the back of the book, and use chalk to trace it onto the fabric two times.

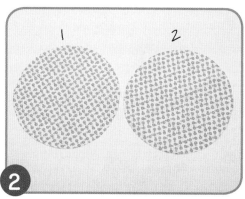

2 Cut out the two fabric pieces.

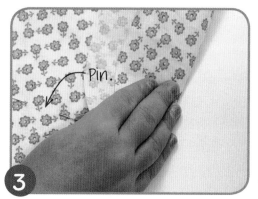

3 Put the fabric together with the good sides out. Use pins to hold the fabric together.

Pin.

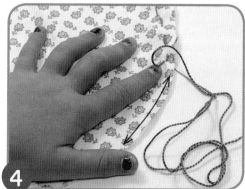

4 Time to sew! Go around the edge with a whipstitch or a running stitch. Leave a hole as long as your finger for stuffing the pillow.

GO TO NEXT PAGE ➡

MAKE IT YOURS

* *Decorate your pillow with buttons or trim.*

* *Use fleece or felt.*

* *Sew with a sewing machine.*

* *Make different shapes and sizes of pillows.*

* *Add a pocket to make a tooth fairy pillow or to hold a Pocket Pal (see page 55).*

Add a button in the middle.

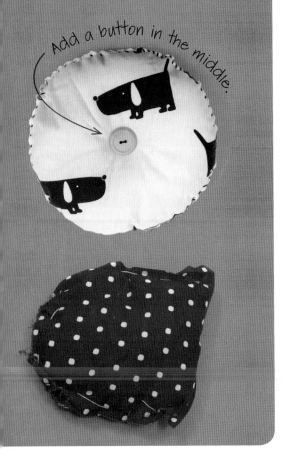

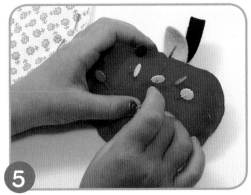

5 Remove the pins and the needle, and put them in your pincushion. Do not knot the end of the thread.

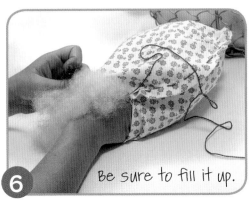

Be sure to fill it up.

6 Stuff the pillow.

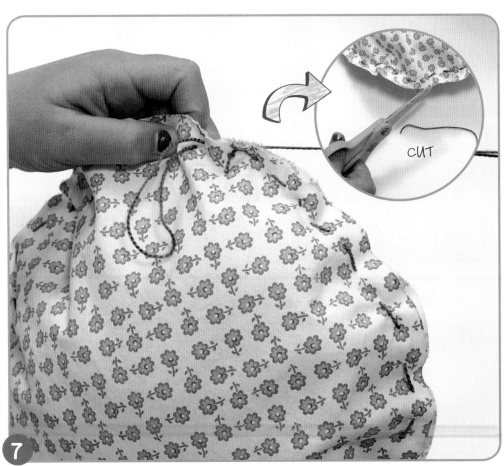

CUT

7 Rethread the needle, and sew up the hole. When the hole is closed, knot the thread. Cut off the end of the thread right above the knot.

You just made a So Soft Pillow!

Stuffies ☆

A stuffie is a one-of-a-kind creature.

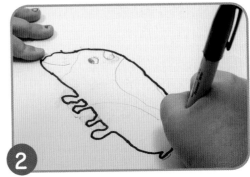

Maggie made a guinea pig because she really likes them. She named it Peach Pie Tangerine.

What You Need

- x Muslin fabric, as big as a sheet of paper
- x Felt or fleece, as big as a sheet of paper
- x Piece of white paper
- x Pencil
- x Black marker
- x Fabric markers
- x Crayons
- x Iron
- x Scissors
- x Pins
- x Sewing needle
- x Thread
- x Stuffing

LET'S REVIEW

Before you begin, you'll need to know how to:

whipstitch (see page 27)

sew a running stitch (see page 24)

stuff a pillow (see page 36)

A NOTE FOR GROWN-UPS

This project allows sewers to use their own original drawings to create unique stuffed animals. Kids can draw the Stuffie directly onto the muslin, but drawing it on paper and then tracing it onto the fabric will ensure fewer mistakes. Sewers might need help cutting out their Stuffie. Be sure they leave a fabric border around the drawing. There's some ironing involved, too, so you'll want to discuss ironing safety.

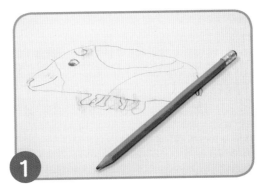

1 Use a pencil to draw a Stuffie on paper. The drawing shown here is Maggie's guinea pig.

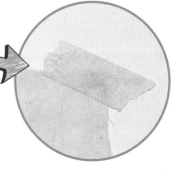

2 Trace the pencil lines with a black marker.

3 Place the muslin fabric on top of the Stuffie drawing. You will see the black marker lines through the muslin. Trace the lines of the Stuffie with fabric markers.

TIP: Tape the muslin to the table so it won't wiggle.

GO TO NEXT PAGE ➡

4 Color the Stuffie with crayons. Now you can see what the guinea pig really looks like. Be sure to color in the whole area.

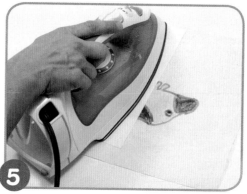

5 Ask an adult to help you iron the fabric. Place a piece of paper over the crayon to absorb the wax. If you don't, the iron will get messy.

6 Pick a piece of felt or fleece to use for the backing.

MAKE IT YOURS

* *Leave the bottom open and turn your Stuffie into a puppet.*

* *Make your Stuffie whatever you want — a doll, perhaps, or even a soccer ball.*

* *Leave the fabric in a rectangle instead of cutting around the lines and you have a pillow.*

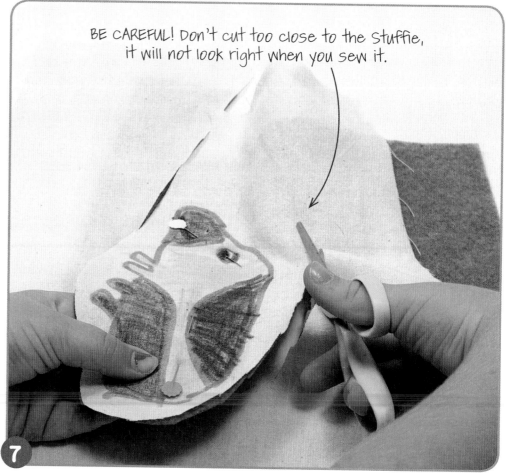

BE CAREFUL! Don't cut too close to the Stuffie, it will not look right when you sew it.

7 Pin the fabric Stuffie and the backing felt or fleece together. Cut around the Stuffie, leaving a border of muslin for a seam allowance.

Remember to leave a hole for stuffing!

8

Time to sew! Sew around the edge with a whipstitch or a running stitch. Leave a hole for stuffing the Stuffie.

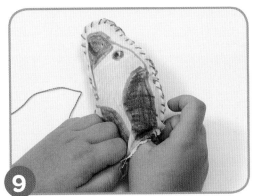

9

Stuff your Stuffie! Remove the pins and take the needle off the thread first.

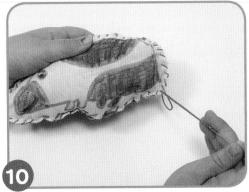

10

Rethread the needle, and sew up the hole. Make a knot and cut the thread.

Now that your Stuffie is done, give it a hug!

"I like making my own stuffed animals because you can use your imagination. You get to choose whatever you want."
— MAGGIE, 7

Your Little Friend ☆☆

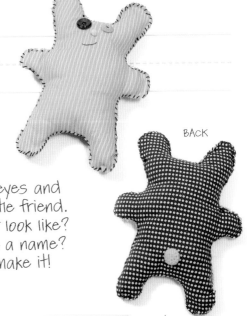

FRONT

BACK

What You Need

- x Pattern for Your Little Friend
- x Cotton fabric, 2 pieces as big as a sheet of paper
- x Chalk
- x Scissors
- x Notions
- x Pins
- x Sewing needle
- x Thread
- x Stuffing

Close your eyes and imagine a little friend. What does it look like? Does it have a name? Now, go make it!

You can use two different kinds of fabric for the front and back.

LET'S REVIEW

Before you begin, you'll need to know how to:

whipstitch (see page 27)

sew a running stitch (see page 24)

sew on a button (see page 31)

stuff a pillow (see page 36)

A NOTE FOR GROWN-UPS

After making a few pillows, kids will be ready to hand-sew a friend to hug (machine sewing is not recommended for this project). Oftentimes when making dolls and stuffed animals, the legs and arms end up too skinny to sew or stuff. The proportions on this pattern work well. Advise sewers to decorate the face and body before sewing the sides together. You may also need to help when it comes to stuffing the arms, legs, and ears.

1 Find the pattern piece in the back of the book, and use chalk to trace it onto one of the pieces of fabric. Now, trace the pattern again onto the other piece of fabric.

2 Cut out both pieces of fabric.

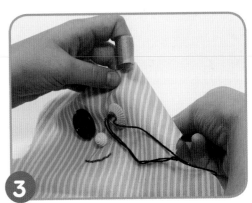

3 Decorate the pieces before you sew them together. Use buttons or other notions to add a face, tail, clothes, and anything else to make it yours!

GO TO NEXT PAGE →

MAKE IT YOURS

* *Use fleece or felt fabric.*

* *Change the shape of the ears, arms, and legs.*

* *Add a tail.*

* *Make it double-sided.*

* *Don't be afraid — make it yours!*

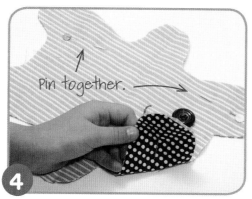

4 Put the front piece on top of the back with the decorated sides out. Pin the pieces together.

Pin together.

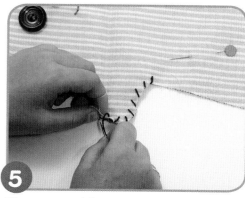

5 Time to sew! Sew around the edge with a whipstitch or a running stitch.

Leave a hole for stuffing.

6 Leave a hole for putting in the stuffing. Remove the pins and take off the needle.

TIP: Use a pencil or chopstick to push the stuffing into small areas.

7 Stuff your little friend. Be sure to get stuffing into all the small areas.

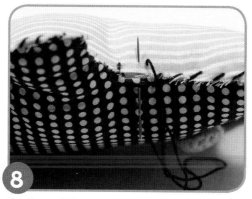

8 Rethread the needle and sew the hole closed. Make a knot, and cut the thread.

Now, say "Hi!" to your new little friend!

Take-It-with-You Blanket ☆☆☆

where will you take me?

What You Need

- x Patterns for the Take-It-with-You Blanket Pocket and the Pocket Pal
- x Fleece, 1 yard
- x Felt scraps
- x Chalk
- x Scissors
- x Sewing needle
- x Thread
- x Ribbon or trim
- x Notions
- x Pins
- x Stuffing

LET'S REVIEW

Before you begin, you'll need to know how to:

whipstitch (see page 27)

sew a running stitch (see page 24)

A NOTE FOR GROWN-UPS

This project has a lot of steps and might require more than one sewing session. Still, with some patience, this is a fun, versatile project! Kids might need help with sewing the legs and arms on the Pocket Pal, cutting the fleece in half, and adding the pocket. Please note that a yard of fleece will yield two blankets.

Part One: Making the Pocket Pal

what a cute face! you can stitch on eyes too, or use buttons or googly eyes.

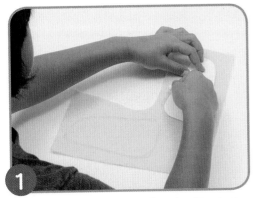

1 Find the pattern piece for the Pocket Pal in the back of the book. Use chalk to trace it onto the felt two times.

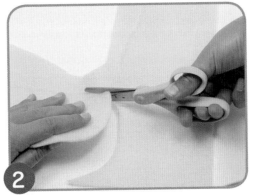

2 Cut out the felt. You will have two pieces of felt for the Pocket Pal body.

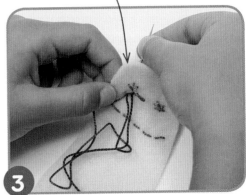

3 Add a face to one piece of your Pocket Pal. Use a running stitch for the mouth.

GO TO NEXT PAGE →

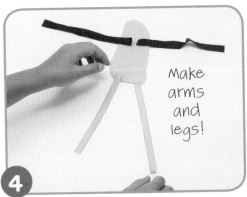

4 Use ribbon or trim to make arms and legs. Cut four pieces. Make them as long as you think they should be. Then lay them on the back piece of the Pocket Pal.

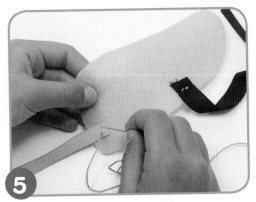

5 Sew or glue the arms and legs in place.

Make ankles and wrists!

6 Knot the ribbon where the wrists and ankles go, if you like.

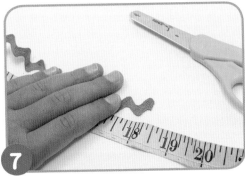

7 Cut a piece of ribbon or trim that is 18 inches long. This is the leash.

8 Sew or glue the leash to the side of the pocket pal.

The sewn ends of the arms and legs should be on the inside.

9 Put the front Pocket Pal piece on top.

GO TO NEXT PAGE

MAKE IT YOURS

* Make your own style of a Pocket Pal. A small Stuffie (see page 49) would be perfect!

* Use a towel or old blanket instead of fleece for the blanket.

* Decorate the pocket before sewing it on the blanket.

* Add a pocket pal to a So Soft Pillow (see page 47), Draw-It-Up Tote (see page 70), or your backpack.

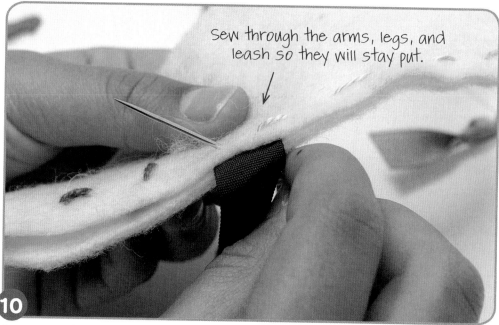

Sew through the arms, legs, and leash so they will stay put.

10 Sew around the edge of the Pocket Pal with a whipstitch or a running stitch. Sew through the arms, legs, and leash so they will stay put. Leave the bottom open for stuffing the Pocket Pal. You are almost done.

11 Take the needle off the thread, and stuff the Pocket Pal.

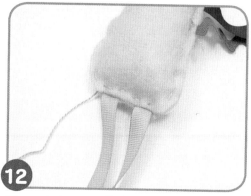

12 Thread the needle back on. Sew the bottom closed. Make a knot and cut the thread.

The Pocket Pal is done! Time to make the blanket.

Part Two: Making the Blanket

1 Fold the yard of fleece in half so that the shorter ends match up.

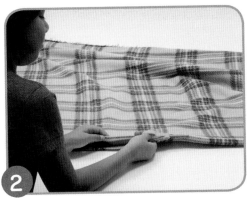

2 Cut along the fold. Take one of the halves for your blanket and save the other one to make another blanket. Trim the edges of the half you are using if needed.

3 Fringe the fleece. Cut slits about 1 inch apart around all four sides.

4 Now make the pocket. Find the pattern piece for the pocket in the back of the book. Trace the pocket pattern onto fleece or felt one time. Cut out the pocket.

Try not to twist the leash!

5 Sew the end of the Pocket Pal's leash to the side of the pocket.

GO TO NEXT PAGE

"If you make this, you'll have something to play with and cover you. It's really good for car trips, when your dad won't turn off the air-conditioning."

— ANNA MERCEDES, 8

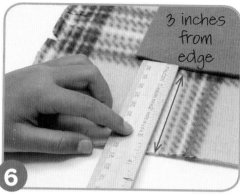

3 inches from edge

6 Pin the pocket on the blanket. Put it 3 inches from the edges.

7 Sew on the pocket with a running stitch.

Put your pal in the pocket! where will you take it?

Story Time

There are plenty of stories in which sewing plays a small part of the story — or, sometimes, a very big role. Here are some books sewing fans will enjoy cuddling up with.

BOOKS WITH SEWING-THEMED ILLUSTRATIONS

* *Mother Earth and Her Children: A Quilted Fairy Tale* by Sibylle Von Olfers, illustrated by Sieglinde Schoen Smith

* *A Stitch in Rhyme: A Nursery Rhyme Sampler* by Belinda Downes

* *Mother Goose Remembers* by Claire Beaton

* *The Princess and the Pea* by Lauren Child; captured by Polly Borland

* *10 Button Book* by William Accorsi

CHAPTER BOOKS

* *Ella Enchanted* by Gail Carson Levine

* *Little House on the Prairie* by Laura Ingalls Wilder

* *The Mary Frances Sewing Book: Adventures Among the Thimble People* by Jane Eayre Fryer

* *Rufus M.* by Eleanor Estes

* *The Tale of Desperaux: Being the Story of a Mouse, a Princess, Some Soup, and a Spool of Thread* by Kate Dicamillo

STORYBOOKS

* *The Brave Little Seamstress* by Mary Pope Osborne, illustrated by Giselle Potter

* *Cassie's Word Quilt* by Faith Ringgold

* *Come Back, Amelia Bedelia* by Peggy Parish

* *Corduroy* by Don Freeman

* *Eight Hands Round* by Anna Paul

* *Frog and Toad Are Friends* by Arnold Lobel

* *Hands* by Lois Ehlert

* *The Josefina Story Quilt* by Eleanor Coerr

* *Joseph Had a Little Overcoat* by Simms Taback

* *The Keeping Quilt* by Patricia Pollaco

* *Mr. Biddle and the Birds* by John Lonzo Anderson

* *Poppy's Pants* by Melissa Conroy

* *The Tailor of Gloucester* by Beatrix Potter

HOLD IT!

In this chapter, you will learn how to custom sew a bag, a tote, a pouch, a wallet, and an apron. Once you've made them, you'll have special places to store all of your most important things.

☆ easy   ☆☆ medium   ☆☆☆ hard

Hold-My-Stuff Bag ☆

PUT GOOD STUFF in here.

This bag will hold just what you need.

What You Need

- x Pattern for Hold-My-Stuff Bag
- x Cotton fabric, 1/3 yard
- x Chalk
- x Scissors
- x Pins
- x Sewing needle
- x Thread
- x Ribbon for a handle

LET'S REVIEW

Before you begin, you'll need to know how to:

whipstitch (see page 27)

sew a running stitch (see page 24)

A NOTE FOR GROWN-UPS

This practical project is ideal for both beginner and advanced sewers. Whipstitching around the top edges is optional; some young sewers may have trouble with this step. Placing the handles at the seam can be tricky too.

Trace pattern piece.

1 Find the pattern piece in the back of the book, and use chalk to trace it onto the fabric two times.

2 Cut out the two fabric pieces.

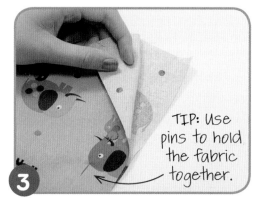

TIP: Use pins to hold the fabric together.

3 Put the fabric together with the good sides out.

Leave top open!

4 Sew the fabric together along the sides and bottom. Use a whipstitch. Leave the top of the bag open. Remove the pins.

GO TO NEXT PAGE →

MAKE IT YOURS

* *Use felt or fleece fabric.*

* *Change the handles — make them longer or shorter.*

* *Make the bag a different size.*

* *Add a pocket.*

* *Close the top with Velcro or a button.*

* *Sew with a sewing machine.*

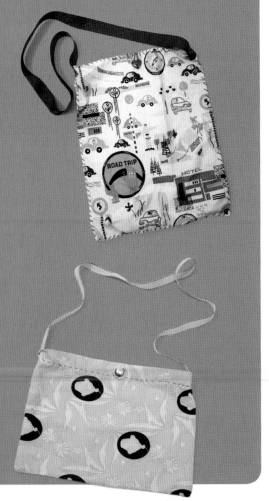

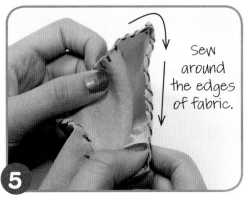

Sew around the edges of fabric.

5

Now whipstitch around the top of the bag to keep the fabric from fraying. Do not sew the two fabric layers together, only sew around the edge of the fabric.

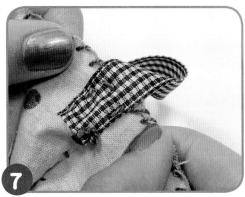

7

Sew each end of the ribbon to the inside of the bag near a side seam.

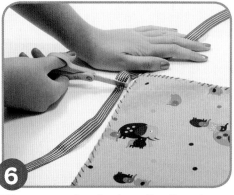

6

Time to make the handle. Cut the ribbon to whatever length you want the handle to be.

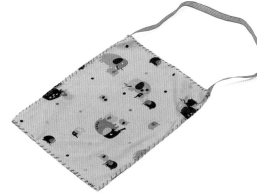

your bag is ready to use. what stuff will it hold?

Wonder Wallet ☆☆

What You Need

- x Pattern for Wonder Wallet
- x Felt, 1 square for the outside and 1 square for the inside
- x Chalk
- x Scissors
- x Button
- x Pins
- x Sewing needle
- x Thread

A wallet is a safe place for important things.

LET'S REVIEW

Before you begin, you'll need to know how to:

whipstitch (see page 27)

sew a running stitch (see page 24)

sew on a button (see page 31)

A NOTE FOR GROWN-UPS

This project is very useful and has many variations. Young sewers might need help sewing on the button. Sewing at the tab can be confusing at first, too.

Trace the pattern.

1

Find the pattern piece in the back of the book. Use chalk to trace the outside wallet pattern onto the felt one time.

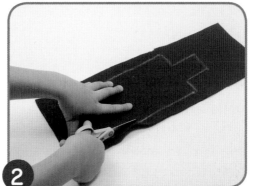

2

Cut out the felt piece. This is the outside of the wallet.

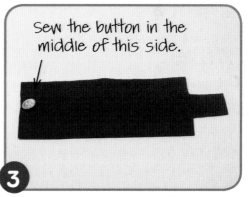

Sew the button in the middle of this side.

3

Sew the button to the middle of the side without the tab. Put it near the edge of the fabric.

GO TO NEXT PAGE ⟶

4 Let's make a buttonhole. Fold the wallet in half. Now fold the wallet so that the tab goes over the button. Feel where the button is under the tab. Mark the bump the button makes with a chalk line.

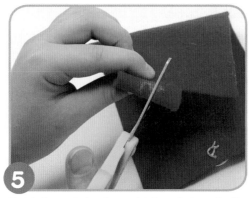

5 Fold the tab in the middle of the chalk line. Then cut along the chalk line to make a buttonhole.

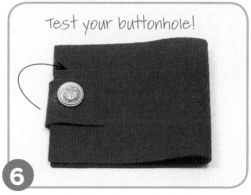

6 Button up! If the buttonhole is too small, cut it bigger.

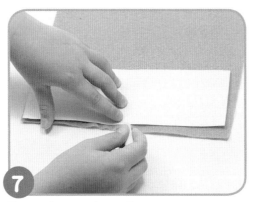

7 Trace the inside wallet pattern onto felt one time.

8 Cut out the felt piece.

9 Pin the inside wallet piece to the outside wallet piece.

TIP: Make sure the button side of the outside wallet piece is facing down.

10 Time to sew! Start at the top corner. Use a whipstitch to sew the outside and inside pieces together along the edges on three sides.

MAKE IT YOURS

* *Decorate the outside of the wallet with your name, embroidery, or felt shapes.*

* *Use cotton or fleece fabric.*

* *Change the number or size of the pockets.*

* *Use Velcro to close the pockets or the wallet.*

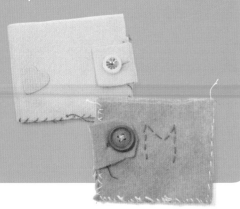

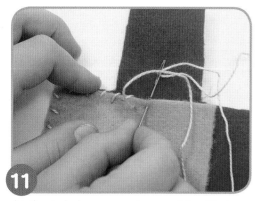

11

At the tab, keep sewing a whipstitch. Push the needle into the outside piece and up through the inside piece.

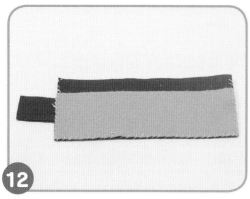

12

All sewn! Don't forget to make a knot. Then cut the thread near the knot. Remove the pins.

"I made a wallet because I needed to put my allowance in it."
— **JACK, 7**

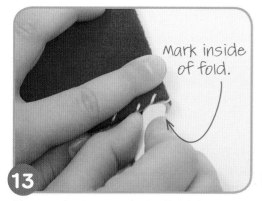

Mark inside of fold.

13

Now make two pockets. Fold the wallet in half. Mark the inside of the fold with chalk.

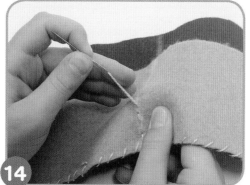

14

Find the mark. Then draw a chalk line up the middle inside the wallet. Sew a running stitch up the middle on the chalk line.

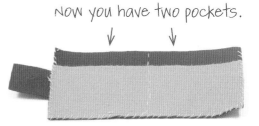

Now you have two pockets.

your wallet is ready for action. what will you put in it?

Draw-It-Up Tote ☆☆

What You Need

- Pattern for Draw-It-Up Tote
- Cotton fabric, ¼ yard
- Chalk
- Scissors
- Pins
- Sewing needle
- Thread
- Large safety pin or a bodkin (see page 14)
- Ribbon, yarn, or rickrack, 2 feet

A tote like this one is great for holding all your loot.

LET'S REVIEW

Before you begin, you'll need to know how to:

sew a running stitch (see page 24)

create a seam allowance (see page 30)

sew a casing (see page 37)

A NOTE FOR GROWN-UPS

This project allows sewers to build on familiar skills and gain new ones. These same skills will be useful in making the My Very Own Skirt project featured on page 110. Kids might need help making the casing and guiding the ribbon through.

1 Find the pattern piece in the back of the book. Use chalk to trace it onto fabric two times.

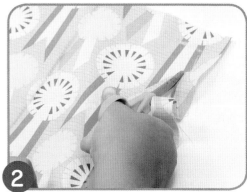

2 Cut out the fabric pieces.

Mark fabric here.

3 Put the good sides of the fabric together. Pin the fabric pieces together to keep them in place.

4 Use the pattern to find where to start sewing. Mark the starting point with chalk.

GO TO NEXT PAGE ⟶

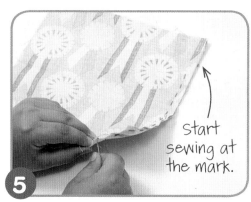

5 Start sewing at the mark with a running stitch. Leave a small seam allowance (see page 30).

Start sewing at the mark.

Leave top open.

6 Sew three sides. Do not sew the top.

Pin down each side of the fold.

7 Time to make the top casing. Fold the fabric down all around the top so the edge of the fabric meets the first stitch you sewed. Pin each side.

8 Sew around the top with a running stitch. Sew close to the fabric edge to leave room for your ribbon or yarn. When you reach the end, take out the pins.

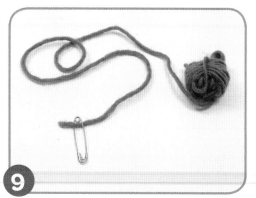

9 Attach the safety pin or bodkin on one end of the ribbon or yarn.

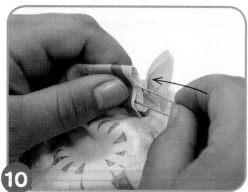

10 Push and pull the ribbon or yarn through the casing.

11 Once the ribbon or yarn is all the way through the casing, cut it at least 6 inches from the bag.

Leave at least 6 inches extra.

12 Tie the ends of the ribbon or yarn in a knot.

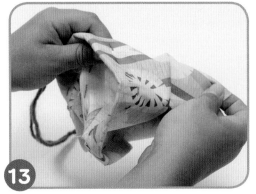

13 Turn the bag right side out.

Draw it up!

Pull the ribbon or yarn to close the bag.

MAKE IT YOURS

* *Change the length of the ribbon for a longer handle.*

* *Make the bag a different size.*

* *Decorate the bag.*

* *Sew the bag with a sewing machine.*

Just-Right Pouch ☆☆☆

LET'S REVIEW

Before you begin, you'll need to know how to:

sew a running stitch (see page 24)

whipstitch (see page 27)

sew on a button (see page 31)

A NOTE FOR GROWN-UPS

This lined pouch requires advanced sewing skills and time to complete. Sewing the buttonhole may be hard for some sewers. For a simpler version, use one piece of felt or fleece and do not sew around the buttonhole.

Button up!

This little pouch is just right for carrying an MP3 player or a cell phone.

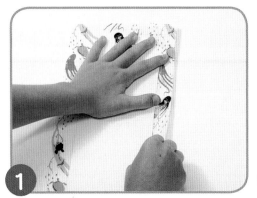

1 Find the pattern piece in the back of the book. Use chalk to trace it onto the outside fabric. Cut out the fabric.

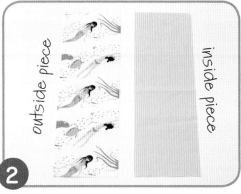

2 Trace the pattern onto the inside fabric. Then cut it out. Here are the outside and inside pieces of the pouch.

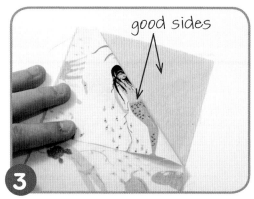

good sides

3 Put the good sides of the fabric together. Pin the pieces together.

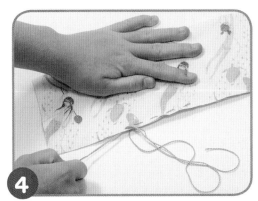

4 Time to sew! Start in the middle of a long side. Sew with a running stitch around the pouch. Leave a small seam allowance (see page 30).

Leave an opening!

5 Leave an opening as big as your finger. Knot the thread, and cut it close to the knot.

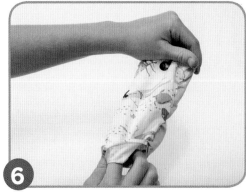

6 Take out the pins, and turn the pouch so the good sides of the fabric are out. Here's how you do it.

Turning the Pouch Good Side Out

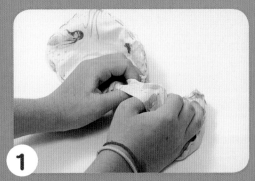

1 Put your thumbs through the opening in the pouch. Squish up the fabric.

2 Use your fingers to push the good side of the fabric out.

Be careful not to push too hard!

GO TO NEXT PAGE

"It's just like turning a sock right side out when you fold laundry."
— LILA, 12

3 Gently push and pull the fabric out.

4 To get the corners pointy, use the eraser end of a pencil or a chopstick to push them out.

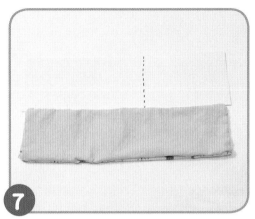

7

Place the fabric next to the pattern. The inside fabric should face up.

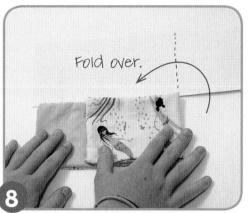

Fold over.

8

Fold the fabric at the dotted line.

Pin on sides.

9

Pin the pouch at the sides.

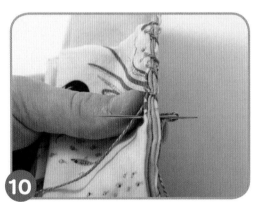

10

Sew the sides together with a whipstitch.

Keep sewing all the way around the pouch!

11

Keep sewing all around the pouch.

GO TO NEXT PAGE

MAKE IT YOURS

* *Skip the inside. Use one piece of felt or fleece instead of two pieces of cotton fabric.*

* *Decorate the pouch before sewing the pieces together.*

* *Change the size of the case to fit other items. Don't forget to add a seam allowance.*

* *Close your pouch with Velcro.*

* *Use flannel for the inside piece of the pouch. It will be extra soft.*

12 Let's add a button. Sew the button in the middle of the pocket near the top.

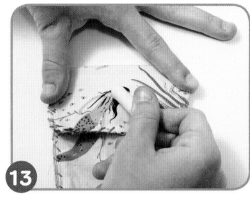

13 Time for the buttonhole. Fold the flap down and mark where the button is with chalk.

cut a buttonhole.

14 Fold the fabric at the chalk line. Now cut along the chalk line to make a buttonhole. Test the buttonhole. It needs to be a little bigger than the button. If it is too small, cut it bigger.

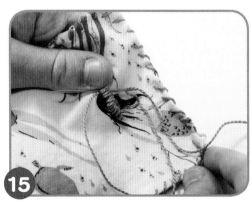

15 Sew a whipstitch around the buttonhole. Make the stitches close together.

After you sew the buttonhole, your pouch is ready to use!

Get-to-Work Apron ☆☆☆

What You Need

- x Pattern for Get-to-Work Apron
- x Cotton fabric for the outside of the apron, ½ yard
- x Cotton fabric for the inside of the apron, ¼ yard
- x Chalk
- x Scissors

- x Pins
- x Sewing machine
- x Ruler
- x Thread
- x 1½ yards double-fold cotton quilt binding or 2-inch-wide ribbon for the tie

Here's an apron to help you get the job done.

LET'S REVIEW

Before you begin, you'll need to know how to:

use a sewing machine
  (see page 29)

A NOTE FOR GROWN-UPS

This project requires advanced sewing skills and may be confusing for younger sewers. You might need to offer help making the pockets and attaching the tie. While ironing is not called for, pressing the fabric and folds (steps 7 and 9) is helpful. In this project, the seam allowance is the width of the presser foot. For an easier version, use a single piece of felt or fleece and begin at step 9.

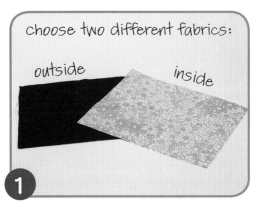

1 Find the pattern piece in the back of the book. Use chalk to trace it one time onto the fabric for the outside of the apron. Then trace it one time onto the fabric for the inside of the apron. Cut out the two fabric pieces.

2 Put the good sides of the fabric together. Pin them together.

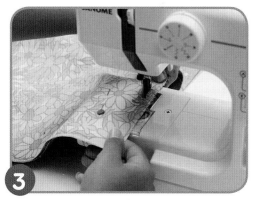

3 Sew the fabric with a sewing machine. Start in the middle of a long side. Be sure to backstitch at the beginning and the end to keep the stitches from pulling out.

GO TO NEXT PAGE →

Leave a 2-inch opening.

4 Sew around all four sides, leaving a 2-inch opening on one of the long sides.

5 Clip all four corners near the stitches.

TIP: Use the eraser end of a pencil to gently push out the corners.

6 Turn the good sides of the apron fabric out through the hole. (See Turning the Pouch Good Side Out, page 75.)

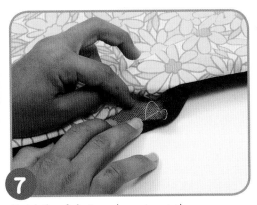

7 Fold the fabric edges in at the opening.

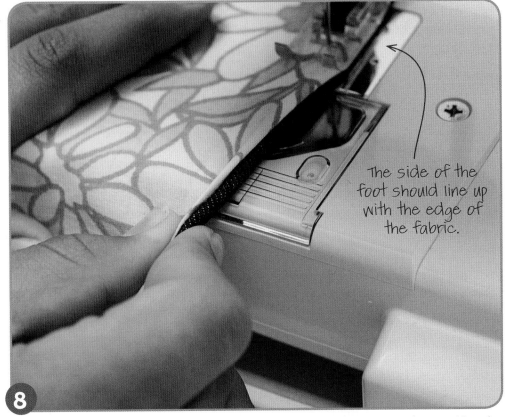

The side of the foot should line up with the edge of the fabric.

8 Sew the side that has the opening. Go right over the opening to close it. Use the presser foot on the sewing machine as a guide.

GO TO NEXT PAGE

MAKE IT YOURS

Design your apron to fit your needs. Maybe you're a cook, a builder, a gardener, or a champion sewer. The pockets can be any size you want to fit all of your tools.

* *Add a small pincushion and you have a sewing apron. Or include a Too-Hot Holder (see page 92) to turn it into a cooking apron.*

* *Label the pockets.*

* *Hand-sew the apron if you don't have a machine.*

9 Lay the apron flat. Put the side you just sewed at the bottom. Now, fold the bottom up. Leave 2½ inches at the top. Pin the folded part.

Leave 2½ inches at the top.

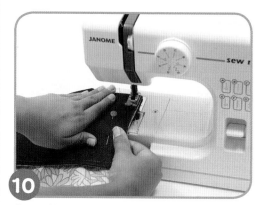

10 Sew all the way up the short sides. Be sure to sew through all the layers.

11 Time to make the pockets. Think about what the apron will be used for. Then draw lines with chalk where you want the pockets to be. You can choose what size and how many.

> "When I grow up, I could be a carpenter, and keep a pencil, a ruler, a flashlight, a screwdriver, pliers, and all sorts of tools in my apron."
>
> **– THOMAS, 8**

12 Sew along the chalk lines.

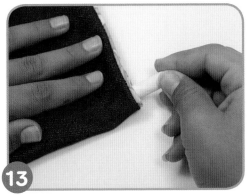

13 Fold the apron in half. Mark the middle with chalk.

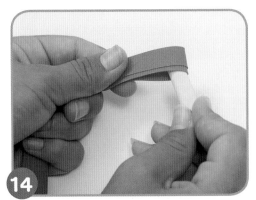

14 Fold the tie material in half. Mark the middle with chalk.

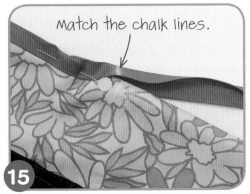

Match the chalk lines.

15 Match the middle marks on the apron and the tie. Fold the quilt binding or ribbon over the top of the apron.

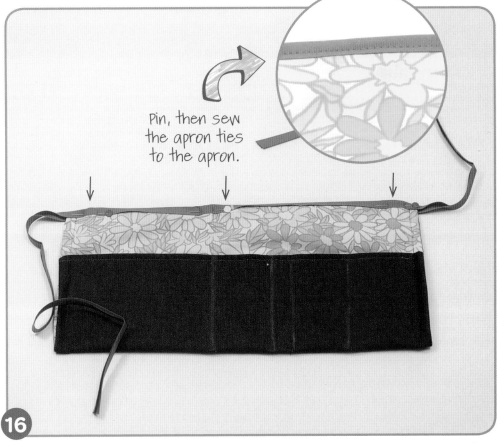

Pin, then sew the apron ties to the apron.

16 Pin the apron ties to the apron. Start at one end of the binding or ribbon, and sew on the ties with a straight or zigzag stitch.

You made an apron! Now, tie it on and get to work.

GIVE

The projects in this chapter are just a few ideas for stuff you can sew and give away to others. Keep in mind that you don't have to make presents that look store-bought. Whoever gets one of your hand-sewn gifts will know every stitch was done with TLC.

☆  **CUTE COASTERS,** *page 86*

☆ 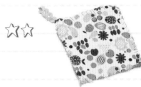 **QUIET MOUSE,** *page 88*

☆  **EYE-SEE-YOU CASE,** *page 90*

☆☆  **TOO-HOT HOLDER,** *page 92*

☆ *easy*   ☆☆ *medium*   ☆☆☆ *hard*

Cute Coasters ☆

front *back*

These coasters will protect the tabletop when people set down glasses or cups.

What You Need

- x Pattern for Cute Coasters
- x Cotton fabric for the tops of the coasters, ¼ yard
- x Cotton fabric for the bottoms of the coasters, ¼ yard
- x Chalk
- x Scissors
- x Pins
- x Sewing needle
- x Thread

LET'S REVIEW

Before you begin, you'll need to know how to:

whipstitch (see page 27) or *sew a running stitch* (see page 24)

A NOTE FOR GROWN-UPS

This simple, thoughtful gift allows sewers to practice stitches. Young and beginner sewers may need help threading a needle and tying knots.

1 Find the pattern piece in the back of the book. Use chalk to trace it onto the fabric for the tops of the coasters four times.

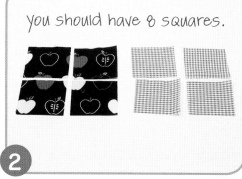

You should have 8 squares.

2 Then trace it onto the fabric for the bottoms of the coasters four times. Cut out the eight fabric pieces.

3 Put one top piece and one bottom piece together with the good sides facing out. Pin the pieces together.

4 Sew around all four sides with a running stitch or whipstitch. Repeat steps 3 and 4 to make the other three coasters.

Now wrap them up!

MAKE IT YOURS

* *Add a felt backing.*

* *Embroider the front before sewing the sides together.*

* *Draw designs on muslin coasters with fabric markers or crayons.*

* *Decorate with trim.*

* *Use scraps and make each coaster unique.*

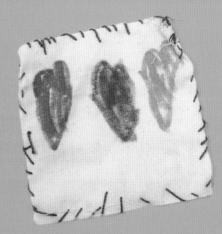

"Give these with some homemade lemonade. It's fun to squeeze the lemons and mix the lemon juice with sugar."
— HATTIE, 5

Quiet Mouse ☆

Here is a little mouse. Who is it for?

What You Need

- x Pattern for Quiet Mouse
- x Felt scraps
- x Chalk
- x Scissors
- x Pins
- x Sewing needle
- x Thread
- x Stuffing
- x Ribbon, at least 5 inches long

LET'S REVIEW

Before you begin, you'll need to know how to:

whipstitch (see page 27)

A NOTE FOR GROWN-UPS

This is a fun beginning project. Sewers may need your help attaching the ears and tail.

Trace the pattern piece.

1 Find the pattern piece in the back of the book. Use chalk to trace it onto felt one time.

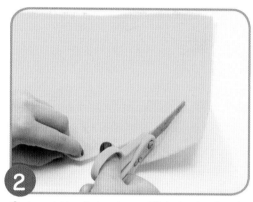

2 Cut out the felt piece. This is the body of the mouse.

3 Fold the body in half. Sew the open side with a whipstitch. Leave an opening at one end.

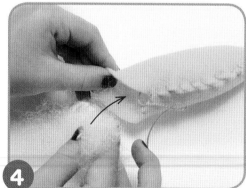

4 Take the needle off the thread. Stuff the body.

5 Rethread the needle. Sew the opening closed with a whipstitch. Make a knot and cut the thread.

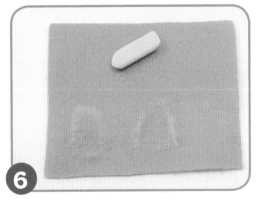

6 Draw two ear shapes on felt.

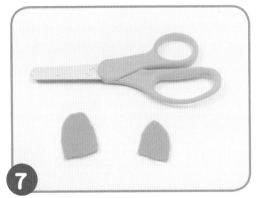

7 Cut out the ears.

whipstitch!

8 Sew one ear to each side of the mouse with a whipstitch. Do not go all the way through the mouse body with your needle. Sew on the other ear too!

9 Now the mouse needs a tail. Sew on the ribbon with small stitches.

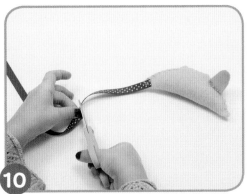

10 Trim the tail to a good size.

you made a mouse!

Give your little pal to a friend before it runs away!

MAKE IT YOURS

* *Use cotton, fleece, or even an old sweater for fabric.*

* *Make eyes with buttons or googly eyes.*

* *Stuff the mouse with catnip and give it to a kitty. Be sure not to use any buttons if you give your mouse to a real cat.*

* *Turn your mouse into a pincushion!*

Eye-See-You Case ☆

Keep your glasses handy and safe with this fun case!

What You Need

- x Pattern for Eye-See-You Case
- x Felt squares, one color for the case and one color for the glasses
- x Chalk
- x Scissors
- x Pins
- x Sewing needle
- x Thread

LET'S REVIEW

Before you begin, you'll need to know how to:

whipstitch (see page 27)

sew a running stitch (see page 24)

A NOTE FOR GROWN-UPS

This gift is perfect for anyone who wears glasses or sunglasses. The felt glasses are optional. If kids want to include them, they may need help cutting them out and sewing them onto the case neatly.

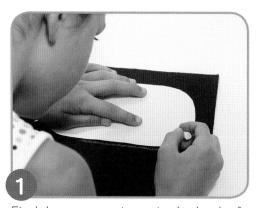

1 Find the pattern pieces in the back of the book. Use chalk to trace the case pattern onto felt two times.

2 Cut out the two felt pieces.

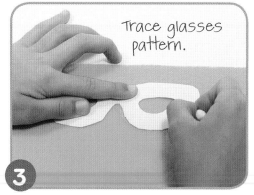

Trace glasses pattern.

3 If you're using the glasses pattern, trace it onto felt one time.

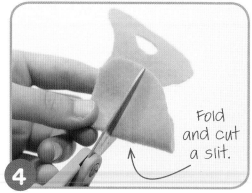

Fold and cut a slit.

4 Cut out the felt glasses. To cut out each eyehole, fold the felt and make a slit with scissors. Now you can easily cut along the line.

5 Pin the glasses to one of the case pieces.

TIP: you can also stick the glasses on with fabric glue.

6 Sew around the glasses with a running stitch.

7 Pin both of the case pieces together. Make sure the side with the glasses faces out.

8 Let's sew! Start at the top of one side. Sew the edges of the case together, leaving an opening at one end. Finish by knotting and trimming the end of the thread.

Test your glasses!

Make sure the open end is big enough to fit the glasses through!

MAKE IT YOURS

* *Put your own glasses design or your name on the case.*

* *Change the size of the case to fit other things, such as a camera or MP3 player.*

* *Use cotton, fleece, or even an old sweater to make the case.*

* *Sew the case with a sewing machine.*

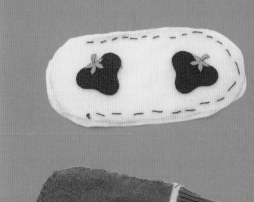

"I like it! It's for your sunglasses."
– **PHOEBE, 5**

Too-Hot Holder ☆☆

What You Need

- x Pattern for Too-Hot Holder
- x Cotton fabric, two pieces at least 8 inches square
- x Felt square
- x Chalk
- x Scissors
- x Pins
- x Sewing needle
- x Thread
- x Ribbon or trim, 7 inches long

Here's a gift your favorite cook will find very handy!

LET'S REVIEW

Before you begin, you'll need to know how to:

whipstitch (see page 27)

A NOTE FOR GROWN-UPS

This is a next-step project for sewers who are gaining experience. Kids may need help pushing the needle through the ribbon and all the pieces of fabric to begin sewing.

IMPORTANT NOTE: The finished holder is not made for handling super-hot pots and pans. Please use this holder for warm items only or as a trivet to set serving dishes on.

1 Find the pattern piece in the back of the book, and use chalk to trace it onto fabric two times. You can use two different kinds of fabric.

you can use two different fabrics.

2 Cut out the fabric pieces.

3 Now trace the same pattern piece onto felt one time.

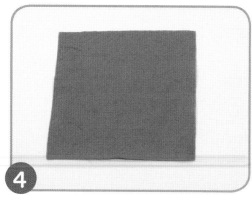

4 Cut out the felt piece.

5

Make a felt sandwich. Put the felt between the two pieces of fabric. Make sure the good sides of the fabric face out.

Fold in half.

6

Cut a piece of ribbon or trim, such as rickrack, 7 inches long, and fold it in half.

TIP: Make sure the loop is on the outside.

7

Put the ribbon on top of the felt. It should be right under the top fabric. Pin the ribbon in place.

GO TO NEXT PAGE

"I made this potholder for someone who cooks cookies and brownies!"
— FRANCES, 7

TOO-HOT HOLDER

First stitch goes through ALL layers.

8 Time to sew! Sew the first stitch through the ribbon and all the fabric layers.

MAKE IT YOURS

* *Make one side of the holder muslin and decorate it with fabric markers or crayons before sewing.*

* *Use holiday fabric.*

* *Sew the holder with a sewing machine.*

TIP: Take your time and make small stitches.

9 Sew with a whipstitch around all four sides. You can pin the layers together so they stay in place.

What a useful gift for your favorite chef!

Wrap It Up

Here are some fun ideas for wrapping your hand-sewn presents with plenty of TLC — that's tender loving care.

* *Use regular scissors or pinking shears (scissors that cut a zigzag edge) to cut a piece of fabric big enough to wrap around the gift. Use craft thread to tie it closed.*

* *Make your own wrapping paper out of newspaper or brown paper. Tie it with bright rickrack or ribbon.*

* *Give two presents in one. Make a personalized Scrappy Art Pin (see page 123). Then attach it to a card or the outside of your package.*

* *Include your favorite recipe with a Too-Hot Holder (see page 92), or make a pitcher of lemonade to go along with your Cute Coasters (see page 86).*

* *Save tiny scraps of fabric and glue them onto paper to make a one-of-a-kind card. Or cut out a fabric heart and glue or sew it onto paper.*

WEAR

Put it on and show it off! We know you've got your own sense of style. Now, when someone asks, "Where did you get that?" tell them you made it yourself.

☆  **SWEET DREAMS MASK,** *page 98*

☆  **HAT ATTACK!,** *page 101*

☆  **SUPERHERO CUFF,** *page 103*

☆☆  **MY DOLL'S VERY OWN SKIRT,** *page 107*

☆☆☆  **MY VERY OWN SKIRT,** *page 110*

☆☆ **MY VERY OWN APRON,** *page 116*

☆ *easy* ☆☆ *medium* ☆☆☆ *hard*

Sweet Dreams Mask ☆

What You Need

- x Pattern for Sweet Dreams Mask
- x Fleece scrap, at least 8 inches long
- x Chalk

- x Scissors
- x Measuring tape
- x ½-inch-wide sewing elastic
- x Sewing needle
- x Thread

Have sweet dreams with this soft mask. It's perfect for getting some rest while traveling or taking an afternoon nap.

LET'S REVIEW

Before you begin, you'll need to know how to:

sew a running stitch (see page 24)

A NOTE FOR GROWN-UPS

This beginner's project is simple and fun. You'll want to help sewers measure the elastic carefully so the mask will fit just right and not be too tight.

"If you try to go to sleep without a mask on, it always takes longer."
— ZEN, 9

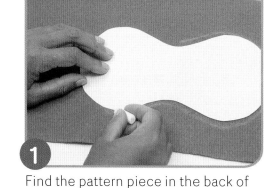

1 Find the pattern piece in the back of the book. Use chalk to trace the pattern onto fleece one time.

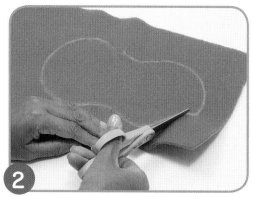

2 Cut out the fleece piece.

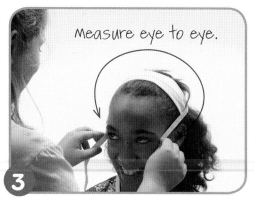

Measure eye to eye.

3 Measure and cut the elastic to fit your head. Get a friend or an adult to help you. You want the elastic to go from eye to eye without stretching.

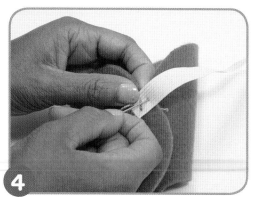

4 Sew one end of the elastic to the inside of the mask. Stitch it to the middle of one side.

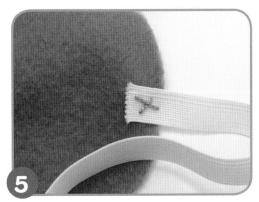

5

Use a running stitch to make an X. This will hold the elastic in place well.

Be careful not to twist the elastic!

6

Sew the other end of the elastic to the other side of the mask.

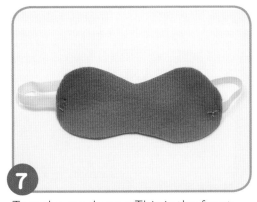

7

Turn the mask over. This is the front.

Now try it on and get ready for sweet dreams!

MAKE IT YOURS

* *Decorate the outside with embroidery or fabric markers.*

* *Use cotton or flannel fabric.*

* *Cut out eyeholes and make a masquerade mask!*

* *Give it as a gift.*

* *Make a matching one for your doll or stuffed animal.*

* *Create Sweet Dreams masks at your next slumber party.*

Hat Attack! ☆

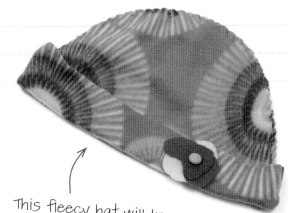

This fleecy hat will keep you warm and cozy on your wintertime adventures.

What You Need

- x Pattern for Hat Attack!
- x Fleece, ¼ yard
- x Chalk
- x Scissors
- x Pins
- x Sewing needle
- x Thread

LET'S REVIEW

Before you begin, you'll need to know how to:

whipstitch (see page 27)

A NOTE FOR GROWN-UPS

This simple hat is quick to make and fits most heads. However, you may have to help your child enlarge the pattern if the hat is a gift for an adult. You can also make the pattern smaller to fit a toddler's or an infant's head.

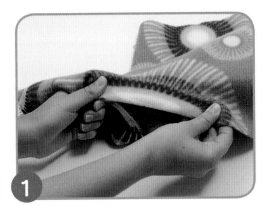

1 Gently tug on the fleece to find the stretchy side.

2 Find the pattern piece in the back of the book. Use chalk to trace the pattern on the fleece two times. Make sure the flat bottom of the pattern is on the stretchy side of the fleece.

GO TO NEXT PAGE ⟶

MAKE IT YOURS

* *Roll up the brim or leave it down.*

* *Add a matching Scrappy Art Pin (see page 123).*

* *Decorate the hat with buttons or pompoms.*

* *Make each side a different color.*

* *Sew with a sewing machine.*

* *Change the shape.*

* *Use an old T-shirt or sweater.*

3 Cut out the fleece pieces. These are the two sides of the hat.

4 Pin the fleece together with the good sides out. The good side of fleece is the fuzzier side.

5 Sew around the curved top of the hat with a whipstitch.

All sewn up! Margaret added a Scrappy Art Pin.

Superhero Cuff ☆

Dress like a superhero with your very own cuff. Emilio made a lightning bolt on his because he can run very, very fast!

LET'S REVIEW

Before you begin, you'll need to know how to:

sew a running stitch (see page 24)

sew on a button (see page 31)

A NOTE FOR GROWN-UPS

This project allows kids to exercise creative expression and provides instant gratification. New sewers might need help with attaching the button and making the buttonhole.

1 Find the pattern piece in the back of the book. Use chalk to trace the pattern on to felt one time.

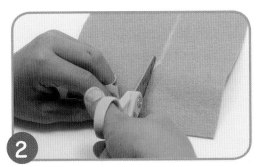

2 Cut out the felt piece.

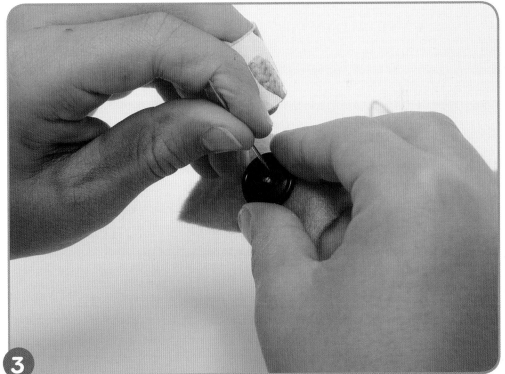

3 Sew the button to one end of the cuff.

GO TO NEXT PAGE →

MAKE IT YOURS

* Decorate your cuff
  however you like —
  try making your own
  superhero emblem!

* Use Velcro to
  close the cuff.

* Glue on felt decorations.

* Make the cuff with
  fleece or cotton fabric.

* Make the cuff longer
  and you have a
  necklace or a belt.

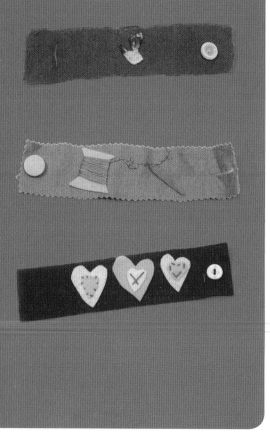

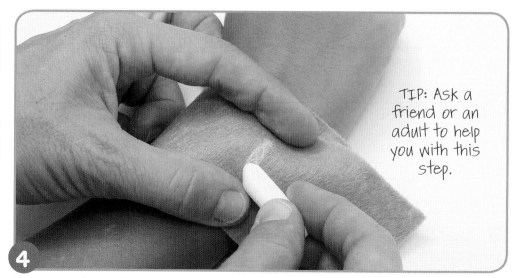

4

TIP: Ask a friend or an adult to help you with this step.

Now wrap the cuff around your wrist. The end without the button should overlap the end with the button. Use chalk to mark the felt where it covers the button. This is where you will cut the buttonhole.

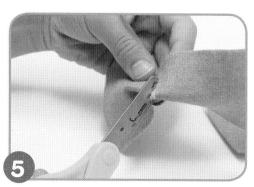

5

Fold the felt on the chalk line. Cut the buttonhole.

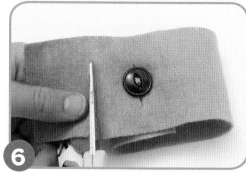

6

Button up! Trim the felt if the cuff is too long.

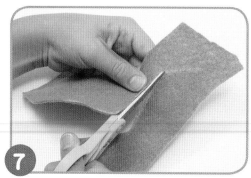

7

Time to be a superhero! Cut out felt shapes for decorating the cuff. Emilio made a lightning bolt.

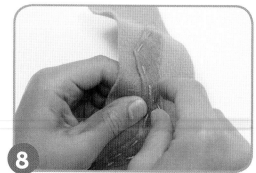

8

Sew on the felt shapes with a running stitch, or glue them on.

Your Superhero cuff is ready to wear!

"If I were a real superhero, my secret power would be transporting. That, or throwing fireballs!"

— HOBIE, 7

It's a bird.
It's a plane.
It's . . . you!

Want to dress like a superhero? Here are four ideas.

1. Make a Scrappy Art Pin (see page 123) to match your Superhero Cuff. Decorate it with felt lightning bolts or other super symbols.

2. Conceal your identity by making a Sweet Dreams Mask (see page 98) and cut slits in it for eyeholes.

3. Sew a special powers cap, using the Hat Attack! pattern (see page 101).

4. Customize a Get-to-Work Apron (see page 79) to make a utility belt that holds all your superhero gear.

Now get out there and save the world!

My Doll's Very Own Skirt ☆☆

That is the cutest doll skirt ever!

What You Need

- x Pattern for My Doll's Very Own Skirt
- x Cotton fabric, ¼ yard
- x Chalk
- x Scissors
- x Sewing needle
- x Thread
- x Ruler
- x Safety pin or bodkin (see page 14)
- x ½-inch-wide elastic, 18 inches long

LET'S REVIEW

Before you begin, you'll need to know how to:

whipstitch (see page 27)

sew a running stitch (see page 24)

sew a casing (see page 37)

A NOTE FOR GROWN-UPS

This hand-sewn project is a good practice run before machine-sewing My Very Own Skirt (see page 110). It is a classic A-line skirt designed to fit standard 18-inch dolls as well as most stuffed animals, and you can easily alter the pattern to fit other dolls. Young sewers might need your help with making the waist casing. While ironing is not called for, pressing down the casing fold before sewing is helpful.

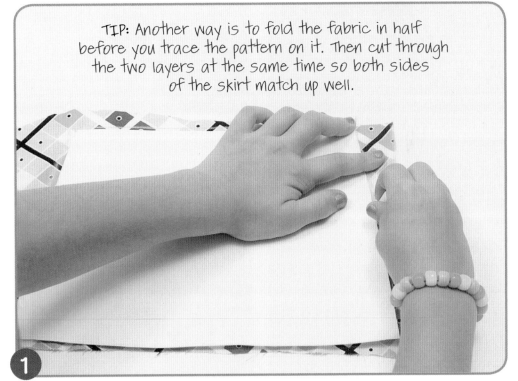

TIP: Another way is to fold the fabric in half before you trace the pattern on it. Then cut through the two layers at the same time so both sides of the skirt match up well.

1

Find the pattern in the back of the book. Use chalk to trace the pattern onto fabric two times.

GO TO NEXT PAGE →

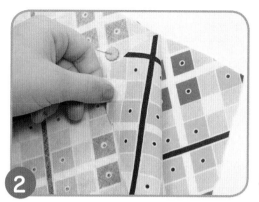

2 Cut out the fabric pieces. Pin one piece on top of the other with the good sides of the fabric together.

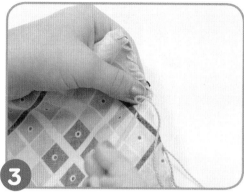

3 Sew both sides of the skirt together using a whipstitch.

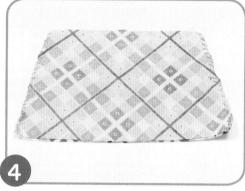

4 Both sides are sewn.

MAKE IT YOURS

* *Make matching skirts for you and your doll!*

* *Sew the skirt with a sewing machine.*

* *Add pockets.*

* *Hem the skirt with ribbon or rickrack.*

* *Make a longer skirt and use ribbons to add shoulder straps. Now you have a dress!*

Fold over 1 inch.

5 Time for the waistband. Fold the top down 1 inch all the way around and pin it in place. The good side of the fabric should face out.

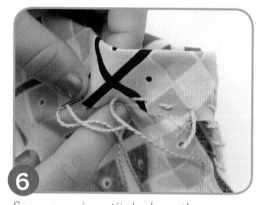

6 Sew a running stitch along the bottom of the waistband to make a casing. Start sewing at one of the side seams. Leave a 2-inch opening.

7 Use a safety pin or bodkin to push the elastic through the casing.

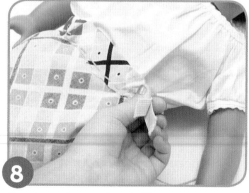

8 Try the skirt on the doll to get a good fit.

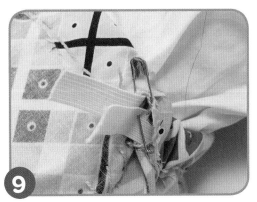

9 Once you have a good fit, safety-pin the ends of the elastic to the skirt to keep them in place while you take the skirt off the doll.

10 Put one of the elastic ends on top of the other and sew them together. Be careful not to twist the elastic.

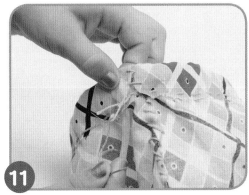

11 Tuck the elastic back in the casing and sew the opening closed.

Turn the skirt right side out when finished.

Stitch around bottom edge.

12 Now it is time to hem the skirt. Whipstitch around the bottom edge, or you could turn up the bottom and sew a hem or add ribbon. Now turn the skirt so the good side of the fabric faces out.

It even fits a favorite stuffed bear.

My Very Own Skirt ☆☆☆

This one-of-a-kind skirt is sewn with a sewing machine. When you wear your skirt, everyone will want to know where you got it.

What You Need

- x Pattern for My Very Own Skirt
- x Cotton fabric (1 yard for the small pattern, 1½ yards for the medium or the large pattern)
- x Chalk
- x Scissors
- x Pins
- x Sewing machine and thread
- x Iron
- x Ruler
- x ½-inch-wide elastic, 1 yard long
- x Safety pin or bodkin (see page 14)

LET'S REVIEW

Before you begin, you'll need to know how to:

use a sewing machine
(see page 29)

sew casings
(see page 37)

A NOTE FOR GROWN-UPS

This A-line skirt is stylish and fun. Still, it can take a while to make, so it helps to break the project into steps. Young sewers will need assistance using the sewing machine and an iron. They may also need help threading the elastic through the casing and sewing the ends of the elastic together. The seam allowance is ¼ inch (the width of a sewing machine's presser foot).

Before you begin, you'll need to decide which of the following pattern sizes is right for you.

SMALL — sizes 5 and 6
MEDIUM — sizes 8 and 10
LARGE — sizes 12 and 14

1 Find the correct size skirt pattern in the back of the book. Use chalk to trace the pattern onto the fabric two times or, for a more even cut, fold the fabric in half and trace the pattern onto it one time.

GO TO NEXT PAGE ⟶

"Wearing a skirt I made is like showing off my sewing to the world."
— TESS, 9

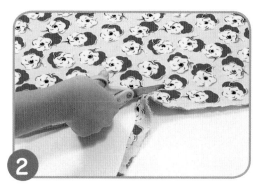

2 Cut out the fabric pieces. If you folded the fabric, carefully cut through both layers at the same time so you end up with two matching skirt pieces. Cutting the fabric this way will make sure the front and back pieces of the skirt are even.

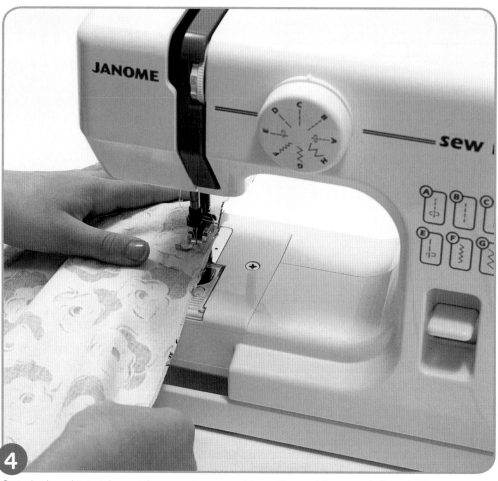

3 Pin the two skirt pieces with the good sides together. Make sure all the edges stay matched up.

4 Stitch the skirt sides with a sewing machine. Sew with a straight stitch.

5 Iron the side seams open. Be sure to ask an adult to help you!

Make the elastic waistband. Fold the top edge of the skirt down ½ inch all the way around. Iron the waistband fold. Again, ask an adult for help!

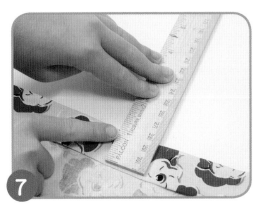

7 Fold the top down once more, this time 1 inch.

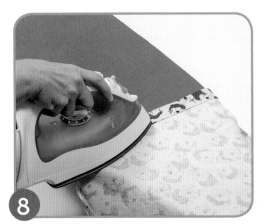

8 Iron the fold with an adult's help.

9 Sew along the waistband casing ¼ inch from the bottom edge. Start sewing at a side seam. Leave a 2-inch opening.

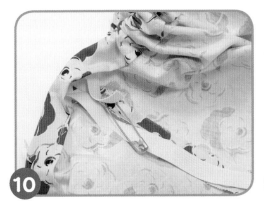

10 Use a safety pin or bodkin to push the elastic through the casing. Take your time.

11 Try on the skirt to get a good fit (see Get a Good Fit on page 114). Have a friend help you. Safety-pin the ends of the elastic to the skirt to keep them in place while you take off the skirt.

GO TO NEXT PAGE

Get a Good Fit

When you are sewing your very own skirt, you can make sure it fits just right. Here's how.

1. Try your skirt on as you sew. Is it too tight or too loose? If the skirt is too tight, you might need to use a larger pattern. Or you might have made your seam allowance too big. If the skirt is too loose, you might need a smaller pattern or a larger seam allowance.

2. Check the waistband. After the elastic is through the casing, try the skirt on. Now have a friend help you pull the elastic so that it feels right. Pin both ends of the elastic to the waistband until you are ready to sew them together.

3. Think about how long you want your skirt to be. Before you sew the hem, try the skirt on to check the length. Remember, the hem allowance is 1½ inches. If you want the skirt to be longer, make a smaller hem.

   Do you want a mini skirt? If so, use chalk to mark the length. If the length you marked is more than 2 inches from the bottom edge, use a ruler and chalk to mark a straight line 1½ inches below the mark you made for the length. Cut along the straight line. Then hem the skirt.

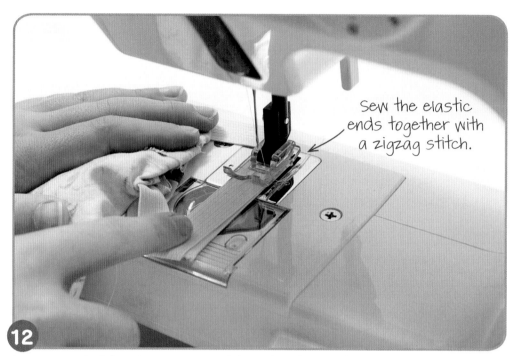

Sew the elastic ends together with a zigzag stitch.

12 Lay one end of the elastic on top of the other. Be careful not to twist the elastic. Sew the ends together with a wide zigzag stitch. If you are not sure how to do this, ask an adult to help you. You can also sew the elastic together by hand.

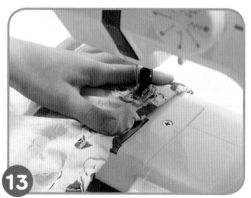

13 Now sew the opening closed with a straight stitch. The waistband is done.

14 Time to make the hem. It is like making the waistband. Fold the bottom edge up ½ inch all the way around. The good side of the material should face out.

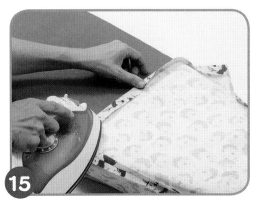

15 Iron the fold. Again, ask an adult for help.

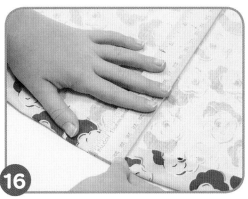

16 Fold the hem up again, this time 1 inch.

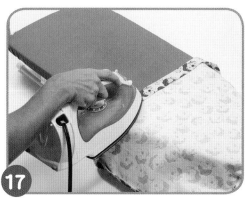

17 Iron the fold with an adult's help.

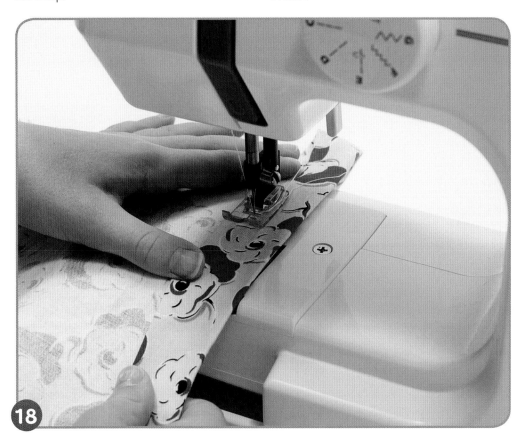

18 Sew the hem ¼ inch from the top. Use your presser foot as a guide. Start at a side seam. This time, do not leave an opening.

MAKE IT YOURS

* *Add a pocket. The Cute Coasters pattern (see page 86) and the Take-It-with-You Blanket pocket pattern (see page 55) are good sizes.*

* *Use two different kinds of fabric.*

* *Change the length of the skirt.*

* *Trim your skirt with ribbon, bias tape, or rickrack.*

* *Sew the skirt by hand. Use a running stitch for the side seams. You can follow the steps for My Doll's Very Own Skirt (see page 107).*

You just made your very own skirt!
Put it on and go show it off to the world.

My Very Own Apron ☆☆

This kitchen apron is made with the same pattern you use to make My Very Own Skirt (see page 110). Put it on, and you'll be cooking up a storm in no time.

LET'S REVIEW

Before you begin, you'll need to know how to:

sew a running stitch
(see page 24)

A NOTE FOR GROWN-UPS

This simple apron comes together quickly. Some sewers may need assistance adding the ribbon tie. For a more finished version, hem the edges by hand or with a sewing machine.

TIP: Unlike a skirt, an apron only needs one layer of fabric. That means you don't have to fold the fabric the way you do when you're making a skirt.

1 Find the pattern piece in the back of the book. Be sure to use your size. Use chalk to trace the pattern onto the fabric one time. Cut out the fabric piece.

2 Fold the apron in half and mark the middle of the top edge with chalk.

3 Now fold the ribbon in half and mark the middle with chalk.

Match the chalk lines.

4

Match the two chalk ma[rks] ribbon to the apron.

5

Sew the ribbon to the apron with a running stitch.

6

Add pockets and trim if you want. The pocket pattern from the Take-It-with-You Blanket (see page 55) makes a good apron pocket.

Tie on your apron, and get cooking!

"Now my clothes won't get dirty"
— GRACE, 8

RECYCLE & REPAIR

This chapter is all about making new items from recycled fabrics and fixing stuff you already have. Here are some tips on turning outgrown clothes into something new and mending the ones you still like to wear. Look around you — fabric is everywhere! You can find lots of new ways to go green.

☆ *easy*   ☆☆ *medium*   ☆☆☆ *hard*

Save-My-T-Shirt Pillow ☆☆

What You Need
- x T-shirt
- x Scissors
- x Ruler
- x Chalk
- x Pins
- x Sewing needle
- x Thread
- x Stuffing

Save a favorite T-shirt that you've outgrown or accidentally stained by turning it into a huggable pillow.

This used to be a T-shirt!

LET'S REVIEW

Before you begin, you'll need to know how to:

whipstitch (see page 27)

stuff a pillow (see page 36)

A NOTE FOR GROWN-UPS

Making a simple pillow out of a special T-shirt that no longer fits is a fun and clever way for kids to recycle. They might need help with marking the size and shape of the pillow. Remind them to plan for the seam allowance when cutting the fabric. If you don't leave enough space, the design might not show well.

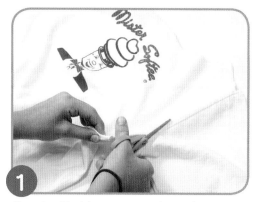

1 Cut the T-shirt apart at the sides, sleeves, and neck. You should end up with two pieces.

Don't forget a seam allowance, too!

2 Decide how big you want your pillow. Use a ruler and chalk to draw the lines on the front piece of your T-shirt. Make sure there is a border around the image you want to show on the pillow.

3 Cut out the pillow shape.

GO TO NEXT PAGE →

MAKE IT YOURS

* *Use two different T-shirts for the front and the back of the pillow.*

* *Back the T-shirt pillow with a different fabric.*

* *Try making a pillow that is a different shape, such as a circle, triangle, or rectangle.*

* *Make a T-shirt bag. Sew up three sides of a T-shirt square and then add a handle.*

* *Turn your old T-shirts into a cozy quilt. Sew a lot of T-shirt squares together using a whipstitch.*

* *Use the leftover T-shirt sleeves to make great headbands or clothes for your dolls or Stuffies.*

4 Pin the pillow shape onto the back piece of the T-shirt. The good sides should be facing out. Cut out the back piece around the shape.

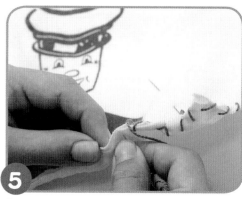

5 Sew around sides with a whipstitch. Leave an opening for stuffing!

6 Leave a 2-inch opening for stuffing. Take the needle off the thread.

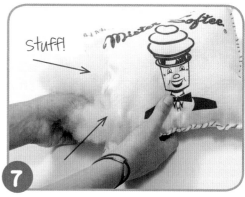

7 Stuff the pillow. Then rethread the needle and sew up the opening.

You just recycled a T-shirt into a pillow!

Scrappy Art Pin ☆☆

This one's called a CRAZY DAISY.

What You Need

- x Patterns for Crazy Daisy Pin
- x Felt and fabric scraps
- x Scissors
- x Chalk
- x Pins
- x Sewing needle
- x Thread
- x Pin back or large safety pin
- x Button

With a little imagination, you can turn fabric scraps into works of art to pin on your clothing or backpack.

LET'S REVIEW

Before you begin, you'll need to know how to:

whipstitch (see page 27)

sew on a button (see page 31)

A NOTE FOR GROWN-UPS

Young sewers can create so many different pins. Encourage them to use their imaginations. Keep in mind that sewing on the pin back may be challenging and require a little help from you.

TIP: Pin the daisy shape on the fabric and cut around the pattern.

1 Find the pattern pieces in the back of the book. Use chalk to trace the three daisy shapes onto fabric. Use a different color of fabric for each daisy.

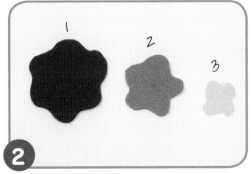

2 Cut out the fabric pieces.

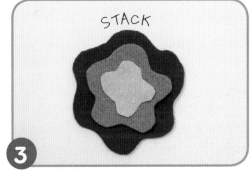

STACK

3 Stack the daisies. You have a Crazy Daisy!

GO TO NEXT PAGE →

4 Sew through all fabric. Bring the needle up through the middle and then back down to the back. Do not knot or cut the thread.

You can use any kind of button.

we used a shank button.

5 Keep using the same thread. Bring the needle back up through the middle and add a button.

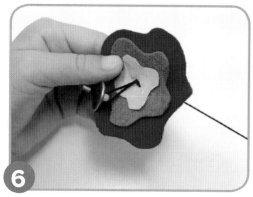

6 Sew on the button. Go through the holes in the button at least two times so it will stay put.

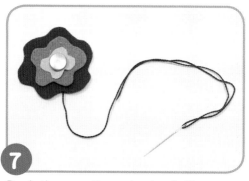

7 Push the needle to the back. Do not knot or cut the thread.

MAKE IT YOURS

* *Try using different shapes, fabrics, and colors.*

* *Create pins to match other sewing projects, such as Hat Attack! (see page 101) or Hold-My-Stuff Bag (see page 65).*

* *Glue your pin together with craft glue.*

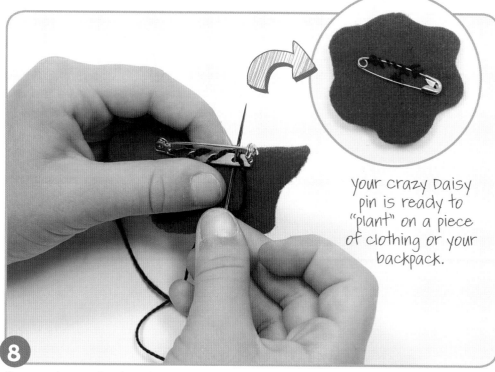

your crazy Daisy pin is ready to "plant" on a piece of clothing or your backpack.

8 Sew on the pin back with a whipstitch. Go through only the biggest daisy. When you are finished, make a knot and cut the thread. Or you can use a safety pin instead of a pin back. Just sew it on using a whipstitch, and be sure to sew the side of the pin that does not open.

Go-This-Way Pin

Here's another pin that is made the same way as the Crazy Daisy, but the shape is very different! You can find the pattern pieces for it in the back of the book.

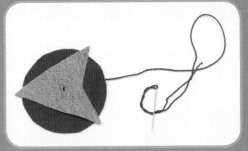

First you put a triangle on top of a circle and sew the two pieces together. The triangle looks like the pointed end of an arrow.

Next, you sew on a button.

Then you sew on a pin back or a safety pin, and the pin is ready to wear. Which way will it go?

Felt Patch ☆

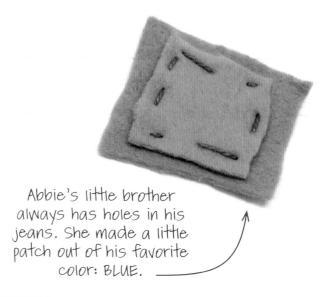

Abbie's little brother always has holes in his jeans. She made a little patch out of his favorite color: BLUE.

LET'S REVIEW

Before you begin, you'll need to know how to:

whipstitch (see page 27) or *sew a running stitch* (see page 24)

A NOTE FOR GROWN-UPS

Mending is a great way for young sewers to contribute to household chores as well as show off their sewing skills. Once they have built confidence with some of the other projects in this book and have mastered basic sewing concepts, they will be ready to mend on their own.

1 Use chalk to draw a patch on felt. Make sure it is a little bigger than the hole you are covering.

TIP: For a stronger and fancier patch, you can cut out two layers of felt.

2 Cut out the felt piece or pieces.

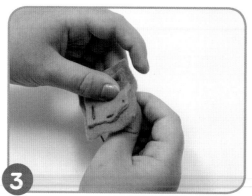

3 If you have more than one piece, stack one on top of the other. Then sew them together with a running stitch or a whipstitch.

4 Pin the patch to the fabric so it covers the hole. Be sure to pin it to one side of the clothes only — you don't want to sew a leg or an arm closed.

5

Sew around the edges of the patch with a whipstitch. Use small stitches so the patch will stay in place.

All patched up!

Adding patches to mend a hole, or just to add style, is fun!

Give Old Clothes a New Look

You don't have to wait for a tear or missing button to fix up worn clothes. Use your mending skills to give your clothes a makeover. Be sure to ask an adult before you get to work!

* *Cut out patches to turn a plain shirt into a cool T-shirt. Patches look great on jeans and bags, too.*

* *Change the buttons on a sweater or shirt. Mix them up for a one-of-a-kind look. Be sure to check the size of the buttons before sewing to make sure they fit through the buttonholes.*

* *Use buttons or ribbon to decorate a skirt, a sweater, pants, or a bag.*

* *Use colorful thread and a whipstitch to sew your name, shapes, or fun designs on your clothes. Sew a whipstitch around the edges of a shirt or sweater for a fancy edge.*

Iron-On Patch ☆☆

Myanne fixed up Phoebe's T-shirt with an elephant patch that a grown-up ironed on. This method works best for covering stains and small holes.

What You Need

- x Cotton fabric scrap large enough to cover the hole
- x Heat 'n Bond UltraHold*
- x Scissors
- x Iron
- x Pencil or chalk
- x Ruler

A NOTE FOR GROWN-UPS

When applying iron-on patches, kids may need help working with Heat 'n Bond UltraHold and with using an iron.

Heat 'n Bond UltraHold is a product sold at most fabric and craft stores. It holds two pieces of fabric together without sewing. See the Resource Guide (page 141) for suggestions on where to buy it.

1 Cut a piece of fabric bigger than the area you want to cover. Lay the fabric on the bumpy side of the Heat 'n Bond. Cut a piece of Heat 'n Bond the same size as the fabric.

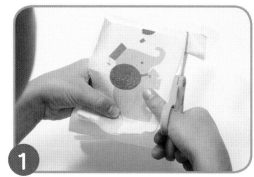

2 Follow the directions on the package to iron the fabric and the Heat 'n Bond together. Be sure to ask an adult to help you.

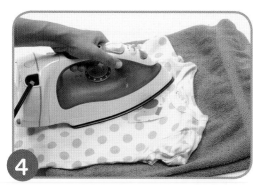

Use a ruler to make straight lines.

3 Now draw the exact size and shape of the patch you want on the fabric backed with the Heat 'n Bond. Cut along the lines.

4 Place the patch where you want it to go. Follow the directions on the Heat 'n Bond package to iron on the patch.

Phoebe's shirt looks even better than before!

Where Oh Where Is My Button? ☆

1
If you can't find the button you lost, look for one you think matches well.

2
Check to make sure the button will fit through the buttonhole.

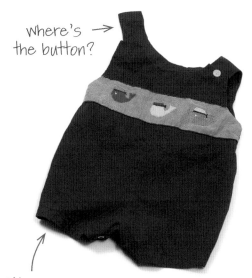

where's → the button?

Little Frankie lost his button, but don't worry. It's an easy fix.

3
Find where the button goes on the fabric. Mark the spot with chalk.

TIP: If there is leftover thread on the spot, cut it off. Be careful not to cut the fabric.

4
Sew on the button. Go through the holes in the button at least three times. Knot the thread on the back of the fabric

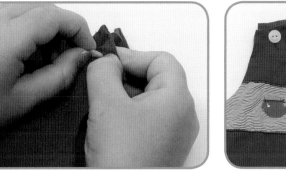

5
Test the button. Now the mended clothing is ready to wear!

Frankie is ready to go out and play!

My Hem Is Falling! ☆

The hem has fallen out.

Sometimes a hem comes undone and hangs down. Don't worry. You can re-hem your clothes and have them looking as good as new.

1 Turn the clothing inside out. Make sure the part of the fabric you need to hem is neatly folded in place.

2 Sew along the fold at the top of the hem with a whipstitch. Go through a little bit of fabric on each side of the fold. Keep sewing all around the hem.

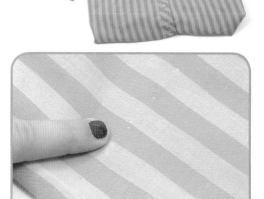

See the tiny stitches on the right side of the shirt? Now the hem is fixed!

Repair That Rip ☆

Sometimes seams come undone. That's what happened with this hat.

1 Pinch the seams together. Sew through both sides with small, close stitches.

2 At the end of the rip, make a knot and cut the thread.

You can hardly tell where it ripped!

Close Those Holes ☆

A holey sweater can't keep you warm!
Sometimes you don't need a patch to mend a hole.

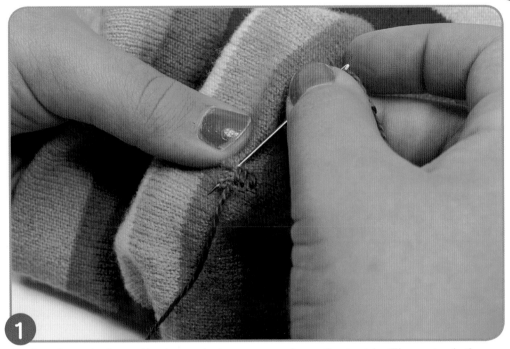

1 Push a threaded needle through the sweater from the inside. Then pinch the sides of the hole together and stitch the edges together on the outside of the sweater.

2 Push the needle back to the inside, and knot the thread on the inside of the sweater. Cut the thread near the knot.

No more holes!

MORE MENDING TIPS

Before you begin, check the area that needs to be mended and think about what you need to do to fix it.

What type of thread should you use? That depends on the fabric that needs mending. For light, cotton fabrics, you might want to use a thin thread like the kind used for machine sewing and a sharp needle with a small eye. For sweaters, craft thread is usually best.

VET CLINIC

Lots of hugs can wear out your favorite stuffed pal. Don't worry! Once you know how to sew, you can be a stuffed-animal vet! Becoming a vet is easy. Just be sure to take your time and use thread that matches your animal's fur. Craft thread (see page 14) is usually best for stuffed animals. Each injury is different. Think like a vet, and use your sewing skills.

☆ HOLEY MOLEY!, page 134

☆ HAVE YOU SEEN MY LEG?, page 135

☆ I CAN'T SEE!, page 136

☆ *easy* ☆☆ *medium* ☆☆☆ *hard*

Holey Moley! ☆

Sometimes all your love will wear a hole in your stuffed animal and the stuffing will poke out. As a stuffed-animal vet, you can doctor it up in no time.

You may need to use a pencil or chopstick to push the stuffing in.

1

If the stuffing has come out of an open seam or another hole, gently restuff your animal. Use a little bit of stuffing at a time.

This is like a whipstitch.

2

Sew the hole closed. Pinch the sides of the hole together. Then sew through the fabric on both sides of the hole. Be sure to make your stitches small and close together.

3

Sew a few stitches past the end of the hole. Make a knot and cut the thread close to the knot.

No more hole!

Have You Seen My Leg? ☆

Like people, stuffed animals can have a broken leg or arm.
If that happens, here's what to do.

"Me and my brother used to play tug-o-war with my bear. One day, we pulled the arms off!"
— CAROLINE, 8

1 Find where the part needs to go. Pin the part in place.

2 Sew on the part. Make small stitches. Sew through the body and the part you are putting back on.

3 It's back on!

Next time, don't be so rough!

I Can't See! ☆

If you have a stuffed animal or doll that's lost an eye, don't worry. You can replace it. It's just like sewing on a button (see page 31), but you don't go all the way through the animal's head. The button shown here is a shank button. If you're using a flat button, follow the same steps. Just make sure you go through all the holes in the button during steps 5 and 6.

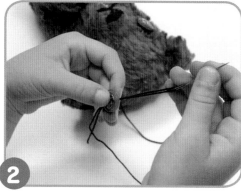

1 Push the needle down and up through a bit of fur where the eye should be.

2 Pull the thread tight. Then put the missing button on the needle and slide it down the thread.

TIP: If you can't find the button your stuffed animal lost, that's OK. Find another one that looks good on your animal.

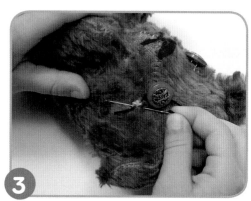

3 Push the needle back in and out of the eye area.

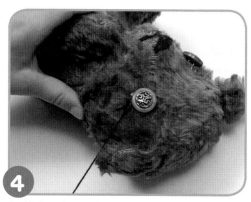

4 Pull the thread tight.

5 Now push the needle back through the button.

6

Sew back in and out of the eye area. For a tight hold, repeat steps 5 and 6.

7

When the button is on tight, knot the thread and cut it near the knot.

That's much better.

Stuffed-Animal Vet Clinic

Now that you know how to help your stuffed animals, you can patch up your friends' animals, too. It's a great feeling to help others! This is also a fun thing to do with a group of friends who like to sew. Here is how to get started.

1. Ask your friends, little brothers and sisters, and cousins if they have any stuffed animals that need some help from a vet.

2. Put the owners' names on the stuffed animals so they can be easily returned. Use tape or little tags for the names.

3. Remember, a good vet is always prepared. Here are some things you should have ready: thread, buttons, sew-on googly eyes, stuffing, fake fur, and felt.

4. Examine each animal to find tears, holes, and other things that need mending. You never know what you might find. Carefully patch up the animals. One time, a stuffed-animal vet had to make a felt cast for a dog that lost a leg!

5. Return the animals to their owners. They will be so happy to have their favorite stuffed animals look as good as new.

"Now you're as good as new!"
— VANCIE, 6

Sewing School Dictionary

BOBBIN — A bobbin is something sturdy you wrap thread around to keep the thread from becoming a big, tangled mess. Look for plastic embroidery bobbins at a craft or fabric store, or you can easily make your own out of cardboard from the recycling bin (see page 20).

BODKIN — This tool looks like a special set of tweezers. It will help you pull elastic or string through a casing. If you don't have a bodkin, you can attach a large safety pin to the end of the elastic or string instead.

BUTTON — A button is an easy-to-sew fastener that comes in two styles. Flat buttons have two, four, or five holes for you to stitch through. Shank buttons have a metal or plastic loop on the back. In olden days, buttons were often made of wood, antlers, or bone. Now, most buttons are plastic. (See page 31 to learn how to sew on buttons.)

CASING — A casing is a long, narrow pocket (or tunnel) of fabric that holds string or elastic. Sewing projects such as a drawstring pouch or a skirt with a stretchy waistband have casings. (See page 37 to learn how to make one.)

COTTON — Cotton fabric is made from the cotton plant. It is easy to cut and sew, but it is also quick to fray. Cotton fabric has a "good" side (see Fabric below), so be sure to pay attention when you're cutting and sewing this kind of fabric.

ELASTIC — You will need this stretchy trim for a few projects in this book, such as the Sweet Dreams Mask (see page 98) and My Very Own Skirt (see page 110). A good size elastic to buy is ½ inch wide.

EMBROIDERY — This style of sewing allows you to draw a picture with your needle and thread. For example, you might use a running stitch and some red thread to embroider a smile on a Your Little Friend pal (see page 53).

FABRIC — Fabric is a material, or textile, that is created from millions of woven threads that are natural or man-made. The "good," or "right," side of the fabric, which is the one you want to show on the outside of your sewing projects, is usually brighter than the other side.

FABRIC GLUE — This is a special kind of glue made to use on fabric. It often works well when you want to decorate a finished project with notions such as googly eyes or pieces of felt. We like Sobo Craft and Fabric Glue.

FELT — This is a thick, colorful fabric that won't fray — and a good material for gluing or embroidering. Felt does not have a "good" side. Felt is often made from sheep's wool, so sometimes it feels scratchy against your skin. You can layer felt with other fabrics when making projects like the Cute Coasters (see page 86) and the Too-Hot Holder (see page 92).

FLEECE — If you want a fabric that is extrasoft, snuggly, and warm, fleece is a good choice. Fleece is a man-made fabric. Because it won't fray, it is also a good fabric to use when you're in a hurry to finish your project. It is perfect for some of the Hug and Wear projects, such as the Take-It-with-You Blanket (see page 55), Hat Attack! (see page 101), and the Sweet Dreams Mask (see page 98).

MUSLIN — Muslin is a thin cotton fabric that is good for drawing and tracing. You will want to use muslin when you make a Stuffie (see page 49). You can also create your own fabric design by decorating a piece of muslin with crayons or fabric markers.

NEEDLE — A needle is your most important tool for sewing. It has an eye, or hole, on one end and a point on the other (see Anatomy of a Needle, page 22). We like to use a chenille size 22 sharp point needle. Its large eye makes it easy for young sewers to thread.

NEEDLE THREADER — Threading a needle can be tricky. A needle threader is a small tool with a thin hook that will help you get the thread through the eye of the needle. Be sure to keep your needle threader with your spare needles. We like the LoRan Needle Threader for large-eye needles. Wire loop needle threaders can break easily when used with craft thread and large-eye needles.

NOTIONS — This includes ribbon, rickrack, lace, beads, sparkles, fabric scraps and trims, and other items you can use to make a face on a stuffed animal or doll. You can also use notions to decorate clothes and gifts.

PATTERN — This is a paper outline of shapes that you need to trace onto fabric and then cut out, before you can start sewing. For some projects, such as the So Soft Pillow (see page 47), you can make your own patterns by drawing simple shapes onto construction paper or the flat part of a brown paper grocery bag. You can trace your pattern with a marker or a pencil, but we like using chalk best because it disappears when you brush it away.

GO TO NEXT PAGE

STUFFING — This is what you need to fluff up a pillow or a stuffed animal or toy. You can buy poly-fill, cotton, bamboo, or wool stuffing. Or in a pinch, you can use fabric scraps or old rags. To learn more about stuffing, see page 36.

THREAD — Thread is a long, thin strand of cotton, nylon, or another material that you use to sew your stitches. We recommend colorful craft thread (also called nondivisible fray-resistant cotton floss) best. The threads don't separate, and it's the perfect thickness for when you're learning to sew. Remember to use the Arm Length Rule (see page 20) when cutting your thread!

RUNNING STITCH — The most basic sewing stitch is a running stitch. You can use a running stitch to attach two pieces of fabric together or to embroider a picture or a design. When it's done right, the running stitch looks just like a dotted line. (See page 24.)

SEAM ALLOWANCE — The space between your stitches and the edge of your fabric is called the seam allowance. Most of the seam allowances in this book are ¼ inch wide. Think of it as a margin for your fabric. Don't sew too close to the edge, or the fabric may fray and your stitches might fall out! If you are using a sewing machine, the seam allowance is the width of the machine's presser foot.

SEWING KIT — For a sewing kit, you can use a box, a basket, or a bag that is the right size to hold all of your sewing supplies (see page 14). A good sewing kit will have sewing scissors, a needle book, needles and thread, a needle threader, and a bodkin or safety pin for threading string or elastic through casings. It will also have a few other tools, such as a piece of chalk for tracing patterns, a ruler, and a pincushion with pins.

SEWING SCISSORS — We like Fiskars for Kids scissors, which are good for small hands and are just sharp enough. Be sure to label your sewing scissors and use them to cut fabric and thread only — no paper allowed, not even patterns!

WHIPSTITCH — You use this stitch when you don't have much seam allowance or when you want to sew two pieces of fabric together close to the edge. When you whipstitch, the thread goes around the edges of the fabric layers. You can also whipstitch a single fabric edge to decorate it and help keep the material from fraying (see page 27).

Sewing School Resource Guide

While you can find many sewing supplies around the house, we recommend that young sewers use a few special tools that are designed for smaller hands. Share this guide with an adult who is helping you learn to sew. It will tell you what supplies you need to start sewing and where you can find them.

Tools and Supplies

All of the materials and tools needed for your sewing kit (see page 14) as well as the other products we suggest, such as Heat 'n Bond and fabric markers, are readily available at most craft and fabric stores.

* **Montessori Services** (www.*montessoriservices.com/store*) has a good selection of sewing supplies for children, as well as lacing and stringing kits for first-time sewers.

* **Create For Less** (www.*createforless.com*) is a good source if you are sewing with a group and would like to buy in bulk.

* **The Janome Sew Mini Sewing Machine**, a kid-sized sewing machine we use with young sewers, is available at **Hancock Fabrics** (www.*hancockfabrics.com*), Home Depot, and many online stores.

Fabrics

Many of the projects in this book use felt. Felt squares are available at craft stores and online stores, including the following:

* **A Child's Dream Come True**
  http://achildsdream.com

* **Felt-o-rama**
  www.feltorama.com

A great number of the cotton fabrics used to make the projects photographed for this book are the creations of designers such as Joel Dewberry, Robert Kaufman, Lizzy House, and Heather Ross. A variety of their printed and patterned fabrics are available in retail stores nationwide. There are many online sources that sell fabric. Following are a few to get you started:

* **Crafty Planet**
  www.craftyplanet.com

* **Etsy**
  www.etsy.com

* **Fabric Worm**
  www.fabricworm.com

* **Pink Chalk Fabrics**
  www.pinkchalkfabrics.com

* **Reprodepot Fabrics**
  www.reprodepot.com

* **Sew, Mama, Sew!**
  www.sewmamasew.com

* **superbuzzy**
  www.superbuzzy.com

GO TO NEXT PAGE

"Keep sewing!"
— MERIWETHER, 6

Blogs for Kids Who Love to Sew

While the following blogs are written for adults, they offer projects, tutorials, ideas, and resources for crafty kids.

* **5 Orange Potatoes**
  www.5orangepotatoes.com/blog

* **BloesemKids**
  http://bkids.typepad.com

* **The Crafty Crow**
  http://belladia.typepad.com/crafty_crow

* **Kleas**
  www.kleas.typepad.com

* **The Long Thread**
  http://thelongthread.com

* **SouleMama**
  http://soulemama.typepad.com

Check Us Out!

Visit our Sewing School blog (http://sewingschool.blogspot.com) for tutorials for young sewers and ideas for sewing with kids, as well as to learn about our own crafty pursuits. We hope you'll share photos of your projects on our site.

Blogs That Inspire Us

As we craft with kids and in our everyday life, we find the blogs listed below to be sources of inspiration. These bloggers beautifully weave sewing in with their daily lives and busy families. While their featured projects are not specific to kids' sewing, many of the ideas could be adapted or sewn by an advanced young sewer with adult support.

* **Angry Chicken**
  http://angrychicken.typepad.com/angry_chicken

* **Chez Beeper Bebe**
  http://chezbeeperbebe.blogspot.com

* **Posie Gets Cozy**
  http://rosylittlethings.typepad.com/posie_gets_cozy

* **Purl Bee**
  www.purlbee.com

* **Sew Liberated**
  http://sewliberated.typepad.com

* **Wee Wonderfuls**
  www.weewonderfuls.com

INDEX

Other Storey Titles You Will Enjoy

Improv Sewing, by Nicole Blum and Debra Immergut.
*A must-have guide has 101 easy, beautiful freestyle sewing projects that
can be created, embellished, and personalized in a single afternoon.*
320 PAGES. PAPER WITH FLAPS. ISBN 978-1-60342-740-1

The Nature Connection, by Clare Walker Leslie.
An interactive workbook packed with creative, year-round nature activities.
304 PAGES. PAPER. ISBN 978-1-60342-531-5.

Nature's Art Box, by Laura C. Martin.
Cool projects for crafty kids to make with natural materials.
224 PAGES. PAPER. ISBN 978-1-58017-490-9.

Recycled Crafts Box, by Laura C. Martin.
Forty great craft projects using materials straight from the recycling bin.
96 PAGES. PAPER. ISBN 978-1-58017-522-7.

Show Me a Story, by Emily K. Neuburger.
*These 40 creative projects and activities will spark the imagination
of the storyteller in kids and adults alike.*
144 PAGES. PAPER. ISBN 978-1-60342-988-7

Trash-to-Treasure Papermaking, by Arnold E. Grummer.
*Dozens of fabulous techniques and projects to transform any paper at hand
— from wrapping paper to junk mail — into beautiful handmade paper.*
208 PAGES. PAPER. ISBN 978-1-60342-547-6.

These and other books from Storey Publishing are available
wherever quality books are sold or by calling 1-800-441-5700.
Visit us at *www.storey.com.*